CAMBRIDGE LIBRARY COLLECTION

Books of enduring scholarly value

History

The books reissued in this series include accounts of historical events and movements by eye-witnesses and contemporaries, as well as landmark studies that assembled significant source materials or developed new historiographical methods. The series includes work in social, political and military history on a wide range of periods and regions, giving modern scholars ready access to influential publications of the past.

Slavery and Freedom in the British West Indies

An active Member of Parliament from 1857, Charles Buxton (1822–71) was the third son of Sir Thomas Fowell Buxton, a well-known and popular philanthropist (several of whose books are reissued in this collection). Buxton inherited his father's interest in social welfare. He owned property in Co. Kerry, Ireland, and became a strong advocate for reform of the Irish Church, and the introduction of a national education system. Buxton also followed his father in supporting the anti-slavery movement. He published this short work in 1860 in response to critics of the abolition of slavery. He argues that abolition in the British West Indies had brought prosperity to that region, and had also fostered the advance of missionary work and Christian civilisation in West Africa.

Cambridge University Press has long been a pioneer in the reissuing of out-of-print titles from its own backlist, producing digital reprints of books that are still sought after by scholars and students but could not be reprinted economically using traditional technology. The Cambridge Library Collection extends this activity to a wider range of books which are still of importance to researchers and professionals, either for the source material they contain, or as landmarks in the history of their academic discipline.

Drawing from the world-renowned collections in the Cambridge University Library, and guided by the advice of experts in each subject area, Cambridge University Press is using state-of-the-art scanning machines in its own Printing House to capture the content of each book selected for inclusion. The files are processed to give a consistently clear, crisp image, and the books finished to the high quality standard for which the Press is recognised around the world. The latest print-on-demand technology ensures that the books will remain available indefinitely, and that orders for single or multiple copies can quickly be supplied.

The Cambridge Library Collection will bring back to life books of enduring scholarly value (including out-of-copyright works originally issued by other publishers) across a wide range of disciplines in the humanities and social sciences and in science and technology.

Slavery
and Freedom in the
British West Indies

CHARLES BUXTON

CAMBRIDGE
UNIVERSITY PRESS

CAMBRIDGE UNIVERSITY PRESS

Cambridge, New York, Melbourne, Madrid, Cape Town, Singapore,
São Paolo, Delhi, Dubai, Tokyo, Mexico City

Published in the United States of America by Cambridge University Press, New York

www.cambridge.org
Information on this title: www.cambridge.org/9781108020695

© in this compilation Cambridge University Press 2010

This edition first published 1860
This digitally printed version 2010

ISBN 978-1-108-02069-5 Paperback

SLAVERY AND FREEDOM.

" MILVERTON.— You are a man in the prime of life. When you were a youth, our great experiment of freeing our own slaves was commenced. I contend that that immense experiment has been signally successful.

ELLESMERE.— For whom?

MILVERTON.— For the slaves themselves, and also for the world in general. If, instead of talking at random about this matter, you would carefully go into details, you will find that, for the most part, my words are amply borne out—that the evils which were liberally prophesied have not come to pass; that the West-India Islands have not fallen into barbarism; that the negro population has not been diminished; that Europe has not been deprived of West-India products; and that, in short, an experiment which no statesman could have imagined to be without considerable hazard has proved, not merely innocuous, but extensively beneficial to the world."

FRIENDS IN COUNCIL.

SLAVERY AND FREEDOM

IN THE

BRITISH WEST INDIES.

BY

CHARLES BUXTON, M.A. M.P.

" Right *never* comes Wrong."

LONDON

LONGMAN, GREEN, LONGMAN, AND ROBERTS

1860

LONDON

PRINTED BY SPOTTISWOODE AND CO.

NEW-STREET SQUARE.

SLAVERY AND FREEDOM

BRITISH WEST INDIES.

A HUNDRED years ago, when black men were seldom seen north of the Tweed, an old Scotch gentlewoman, meeting a negro in the street, cast up her eyes and hands, exclaiming, "Hech, sirs, what canna be made for the penny!" And well might the British people do the same. At a cost, not of one penny, but of five thousand million pennies, we have produced that curious specimen of the human race, the free negro of the West Indies. Such was the outlay. Now, what is the result? What sort of thing have we got for our money? Was that a wise investment of capital?

The reply of some high authorities has been given, and is this — Our islands, they say, the richest and loveliest in the world, are fallen from wealth to ruin; crumbling, deserted, desolate towns; empty harbours; trade gone; agriculture at death's door; the old staples vanished away. The owners of these once fertile lands languishing in poverty, or dead of broken hearts. The negroes, for whom all was done, " sunk

B

up to the ears in pumpkin," growing every day more
savage, more idle, more beastly. Such, they tell us,
is the work that our philanthropy has worked out
under the sun. Is that so, or is it not so? The subject deserves some thought. England's giving freedom to her slaves was an act unique in the history of
man. We know not where an example can be found
of so noble a sacrifice, made by a whole people. As
to its prudence, some may think one thing, and some
another; but no man can lay it at the door of any
selfish feeling. The people of the United Kingdom
thought slavery cruel. It seemed to them a breach
of the law of love which the gospel of Christ had laid
down. For these reasons, and for these alone, they
made up their minds to be rid of it. But they were
not hurried away by their zeal. They chose to pay
the cost themselves. And 20,000,000*l.* was paid
down by them, to get the slaves set free. To us, who
saw this done, it may seem an everyday affair. But
seen from afar, in the coming ages, it may strike men
as sublime.

And was it, after all, an act of shining folly? Has
it really wrought woe and not weal in the world?
Are we to be warned by it against giving way to the
impulses of good feeling? Is the Christian faith to
be found guilty of misleading us into a gross blunder?
It is worth while to find out the true reply to these
questions. For if all this were so, then that noble
old maxim, that "Right never comes wrong," would
be overthrown. Here we have a nation plainly
setting itself to do right, "because right was right;"
because it thought more of what was due to God and

man, than of itself. Has this been a failure, has this done harm and not good, then it may be *unwise to do right.* Wrong, perhaps, might as well be kept going. The laws of God and the rights of man may be well enough in their way, but should we obey the one, or observe the other, we may find ourselves made fools of.

Now we are far indeed from denying that the owners of West Indian property have gone through a time of deep distress. The cry of despair that rose from them in 1847, and the next years, was appalling. Many and many a family once blessed with opulence sank into utter poverty, while hundreds of others had their fortunes shattered if not destroyed. No wonder such an overthrow should have been loudly noised, not only through England, but through the world, and that emancipation should be looked upon as having given the death-blow to our once thriving colonies. People were not likely to bear in mind that, however sad these events might be, still they arose fourteen years after slavery (ten years after the apprenticeship) had been done away, and at once upon a change of a wholly different kind. Nor could they have been expected to remember that the cries of distress came not from the whole population of those islands, but mainly from the proprietors living in England, whose voice therefore rang the louder, but might not be the voice of the mass of the people. It was natural for the world to think that the whole of our sugar colonies were sinking into ruin, though the outcry came from some of them, but not from others. It was natural for the world to think that when it no longer heard " that most outrageous, dreadful, yelling

cry " (to quote the Faërie Queen), it was hushed in
death, though in truth it ceased because the pinch
was over. No wonder the world fancies that our
sugar colonies are as good as swept off the face of the
earth, though in fact they are swiftly becoming a gem
in the British crown, of higher value than they ever
were before.

A long and thorough investigation of the case has
borne us irresistibly to the conclusion, that in those
assumptions the world has been wrong ; and if the
reader will go with us through the following pages,
we think he will agree with us in believing that, even
if we set aside all thoughts but thoughts of pounds,
shillings, and pence—as a dry question of economy
emancipation has *paid*—that it was an act of prudence
for which we, as a nation of shopkeepers, need not
blush before that golden god, whom we are thought
to worship so eagerly. We shall bring forward, what
seem to us conclusive reasons for the persuasion, that
had England not cared a jot for those noble principles
that really nerved her to the work, had she only kept a
shrewd look-out for the main chance, it was not weak
but wise of her to free her slaves.

This, then, is the plain question to which we have
sought out the reply. Taking no thought, for the
nonce, of humanity, morality, Christianity — looking
to the pocket alone — has emancipation answered, or
been a blunder? Good and kindly meant as it un-
doubtedly was, is the world the worse off for it, or
the better off for it? Did the philanthropists ruin
the West Indies? or did they save the West Indies
from imminent, irretrievable ruin, and set them on the

road to a prosperity at once sound and splendid?
Let that be the test of the great experiment of 1834.
Has it plunged the former slave colonies into hopeless
ruin, then never mind its nobleness, let it stand condemned. But if the distress which fell on the West
Indies in 1847 can be clearly traced to other causes;
if it was only a passing storm; if, those other causes
being spent, freedom is now working out a well-being
that was unknown in the days of slavery — then, we
say, let emancipation stand approved in the sight of
all the world.

And this it is which the facts before us seem to
prove. They show that slavery was bearing our
colonies down to ruin with awful speed; that had it
lasted but another half century, they must have sunk
beyond recovery. On the other hand, that now under
freedom and free trade, they are growing day by day
more rich in wealth; with spreading trade, with improving agriculture, with a more educated, industrious, and virtuous people; while the comfort of the
quondam slaves is increased beyond the power of
words to portray.

Never was a more radical revolution made in the
fortunes of a whole people, than when the 800,000
British negroes stepped from slavery into freedom.
When the clock began to strike twelve on the night
of July 31, 1834, they were, in the eye of the law,
things, chattels, beasts of burden, the mere property
of others. When it had ceased to sound, they were
for the first time, not only free-men but *men;* standing on the same level as those who had formerly
owned them. The whole form of things became so

thoroughly new, that it is now no easy matter to
paint oneself a living picture of a state of society
which has been so utterly swept away; but of its
more salient features hints enough remain. And we
must say that in glancing through the piles of information on the state of the slave colonies that accumu-
lated during the anti-slavery struggle, we have been
amazed at the breadth and depth of the cruelty which
slavery was shown to beget. We had been fain to
jog along with the easy and pleasant belief that the
plantations had been under kindly government, and
that the tales of barbarity that used to be rife years
and years ago, were for the most part mere wind.
We have had but too much reason to change our
minds on this head. And yet, though the shadows
of slavery were dark, and too often terrible, there
seems to have been a good play of sunlight upon it
as well; and, luckily, a charming picture of the bright
side of slavery has been preserved for us by "Monk"
Lewis, who was not only a man of poetical feeling,
but of a most kind nature, and who went to see his
estates mainly from a sense of duty towards his slaves.
And truly the life he portrays might seem to have
had in it a taste of a happier world. He reached
Jamaica on the 1st of January (1816), the severe
work of crop time just over, and the negroes at their
best and merriest. The air was delicious. The
fragrance of the sweet wood and other scented trees
put him in mind of the "buxom air, embalmed with
odours" of Paradise, while the scenery was highly
picturesque, from the lively green of the trees and
shrubs, and the hermitage-like appearance of the

negro buildings, all situated in little gardens, and
embosomed in sweet-smelling shrubberies. The joy
of the slaves at seeing massa, if not deep, was at least
noisy. They sang, danced, shouted, and tumbled
over each other, and rolled about on the ground,
while every man, woman, and child chattered its
loudest. The mothers held up their little shining
black imps, grinning from ear to ear, with "Look,
massa, look here; him nice lilly neger for massa."
Nor was female loveliness wanting to complete the
picture; but was well represented by Mary Wiggins,
whose complexion had no yellow in it; teeth ad-
mirable, eyes mild and bright, and a face merely
broad enough to give it "all possible softness and
grandness of contour." Many old servants of the
family (which at that time lived on the estate) came
to see him, and showed such warmth and enthusiasm,
that after the cold manners of England the contrast
was infinitely agreeable, and his heart expanded in the
sunshine of the kind looks and words which met him
at every turn, and seemed to wait for his smiles as
anxiously as if they were so many diamonds.

On three sides the landscape was bounded by
purple mountains, and the variety of occupations
going on all around gave an inconceivable air of life
and animation to the whole scene, especially as all
those occupations looked cleanly. The tradespeople
were dressed in jackets and trowsers, either white,
or of red and sky-blue stripe. Here a band of
negroes carrying the ripe canes on their heads to the
mill; another set conveying away the *trash*, after the
juice had been extracted; flocks of turkeys shelter-

ing from the heat under the trees; the river filled
with ducks and geese; the coopers and carpenters
hammering at the puncheons; carts drawn, some by
six, some by eight oxen, bringing loads of Indian
corn from the fields; the black children gathering it
into the granary, or quarrelling with pigs as black as
themselves, who were equally busy in stealing the
corn whenever the children were looking another
way: such was the scene which met Mr. Lewis's eyes
as he stood in his verandah; and, " in short," he
adds, "a plantation possesses all the movement and
interest of a farm, without its dung, and its stench,
and its dirty accompaniments."

If the mid-day scene was so cheerful, still more
gay and amusing was the one when the morning rose
with tropical suddenness, and all nature seemed to
awake at the same moment. Instantly everything
was in motion: the negroes tramping to the field;
the cattle driving to pasture; the pigs and the poultry
pouring out from their hutches; the old women pre-
paring food on the lawn for the pickanninnies, — all
seemed to be going to their employment, none to their
work; the men and the women just as quietly and
leisurely as the pigs and the poultry. Nor did they
hold their owner in any dread. Just for the fun of a
good chat they would often come and make some
unreasonable request; and on receiving a plump
refusal would go away perfectly satisfied, and " Tank
massa for dis here great indulgence of talk." One
day —

" My friend Strap, the Eboe, came up to the house
dressed in his best clothes, to show me his seven children;

he marched at their head in all the dignity of paternal pride. He begged me particularly to notice two fine little girls, who were twins. I told him that I had seen them already. 'Iss! iss! massa see um;' he said; 'but massa no *admire* um enough yet.' Upon which I fell to admiring them, tooth and nail; and the father went away quite proud and satisfied."

Such was the Arcadian felicity of a slave plantation under the eye of a kind and opulent owner. But it would seem that even such an Eden as this shared the lot of the rest of the earth, of which the angel tells us —

> "Es wechselt Paradieses helle
> Mit tiefer schauervoller Nacht."

For though under the mild sway of Mr. Lewis all flowed so sweetly, by degrees he found things out that did not please him. Nay, his own way of putting it is, that "nothing could equal" his "anger and surprise" when he discovered what had been going on before his coming was looked for. His father had always filled his letters with the most positive orders for the good treatment of the slaves, and had chosen a first-rate agent. Yet this man, from mere sloth, had let an overseer treat them so savagely that at one time " they had been driven absolutely into rebellion, and almost every slave of respectability had been compelled to become a runaway." . . . . " If I had not come to Jamaica myself," he adds, " in all probability I should never have had the most distant idea *how abominably the poor creatures had been ill-used.*"

Day after day, too, slaves on the estates hard by,

hearing of his kindliness, came to tell him of their cruel usage, in hopes he could shield them. For example,—

"*Jan.* 24.—On my return to the house, I found two women belonging to a neighbouring estate, who came to complain of cruel treatment from their overseer, and to request me to inform their trustee how ill they had been used, and see their injuries redressed. They said, that having been ill in the hospital, and ordered to the field while they were still too weak to work, they had been flogged with much severity (though not beyond the limits of the law); and my head driver, who was less scrupulously delicate than myself as to ocular inspection of Juliet's person (which Juliet, to do her justice, was perfectly ready to submit to in proof of her assertions), told me that the woman had certainly suffered greatly; the other, whose name was Delia, was but just recovering from a miscarriage, and declared openly that the overseer's conduct had been such, that nothing should have prevented her running away long ago if she could but have had the heart to abandon a child which she had on the estate. Both were poor feeble-looking creatures, and seemed very unfit subjects for any severe correction."

Vexations at home were not wanting either. His own agent said nothing plainly, but shook his head, and gave poor Lewis evidently to understand that the slaves could not be governed without the cart-whip. In fact, the need of that stimulus soon grew plain, for the production of sugar fell from thirty-three hogsheads a week, before his coming, down to thirteen! "The negroes certainly are perverse beings," is the reflection he makes thereupon. And he was not long in finding that whites are "perverse beings" too, for some alarmed planters actually

wanted the grand jury at Montego Bay to prosecute
him for over-indulgence to his own slaves!

Worse still remained. At his first visit to Jamaica he did not go to his other estate; but " I contented myself," he says, " by impressing on the mind
of my agent, *who, I am certain, is a most humane
and intelligent man,* my extreme anxiety for the abolition of the cart-whip; and I had the satisfaction of
hearing from him that for a long time it had never
been used more than perhaps twice in a year, and
then only very slightly, and for some flagrant offence."
On his return to Jamaica he visited this estate. " I
expected to find it a perfect paradise. I found it
a hell upon earth." The fact was that, although the
agent was in all truth a most humane man, yet, like
the agent of the other estate, and like the rest of
mankind, he saw no harm in what was familiar to his
eyes; and so the eight book-keepers and drivers were
wreaking their will on the wretches under them, and
treating them with " atrocious brutality." Lewis put
things square for the time (though he did not send off
the agent), and when he left he was loudly cheered
by his sable attendants, the tears running down many
of their cheeks, and all thanking him for the protection he had given them, and praying for his speedy
return.

We cannot help wishing that this lively picture of
slavery as it really was, had been given to the world
while the anti-slavery struggle was still going on.*
Those who looked on the slave-owners as villains, and

* It was only published a few years ago.

who thought that at its best slavery must be atrocious, might have learnt from it how cheerful it could
be under a warm-hearted proprietor, who saw to
things himself. And those, again, who would have it
that tales of cruelty on the sugar estates were mere
inventions, that the negroes were the happiest of
mankind; that the use of the whip was unknown,
and so forth, might have caught glimpses of the fear-
ful hue with which slavery was clouded, when the
master's eye was withdrawn, and there was no check
on the agent; who, moreover, however kindly himself, might leave his white and black subordinates to
exercise "atrocious brutalities" without any kind of
restraint. As Lewis observes,—

"The negro has been left entirely at the mercy of the
overseer, who, if he was a humane man, punished him
slightly, and if a tyrant, heavily; nay, very often the
quantity of punishment depended upon the time of day
when the offence was made known. If accused in the morning, when the overseer was in cold blood and in good
humour, a night's confinement in the stocks might be
deemed sufficient ; whereas, if the charge was brought when
the superior had taken his full proportion of grog or
sangaree, the very same offence would be visited with
thirty-nine lashes."

And what was meant by thirty-nine lashes we
must by no means forget. We are sorry to harass
our readers' feelings; but we have taken in hand to
weigh things present, against things past, in the
West Indies. How can we do so, if we cover up
the badness of those bad old times ? Moreover, it
ought to be known in the United States, that the

very same things used to be boldly said here, that
now are said there, as to the mildness of slavery, and
its freedom from cruelty. And yet here is a glimpse,
a brief but a clear glimpse, into the things that went
on, where the slaves did not happen to enjoy the rare
advantage of a humane and resident owner, who
would neither do cruelty himself, nor suffer it to be
done by others.

The following are extracts from a very plain, un-
varnished account written by Mr. Whitely, who was
book-keeper (clerk) on the New Ground Plantation,
near St. Ann's Bay, in Jamaica, in 1832.

He mentions that, on his arrival, he was struck by
observing the great regularity and apparent good
humour with which some negro coopers were working in the yard. While the overseer and he were
chatting on their comfortable condition, some drivers
came up, bringing six field hands who were to be
flogged. The scene that ensued is thus vividly described:—

"The first of these field negroes was a man of
about thirty-five years of age. He was what is called
a pen-keeper or cattle-herd; and his offence was having suffered a mule to go astray. At the command
of the overseer he proceeded to strip off part of his
clothes, and laid himself flat on his belly, his back
being uncovered. One of the drivers then commenced
flogging him with the cart-whip. The whip is about
two feet long, with a short stout handle, and is an
instrument of terrible power. It is whirled by the
operator round his head, and then brought down with
a rapid motion of the arm upon the recumbent victim,

causing the blood to spring at every stroke. When
I saw this spectacle, now for the first time exhibited
before my eyes, with all the revolting accompaniments, and saw the degraded and mangled victim
writhing and groaning under the infliction, I felt
horror-struck. I trembled and turned sick; but, being
determined to see the whole to an end, I kept my
station at the window. The sufferer, writhing like a
wounded worm every time the lash cut across his
body, cried out, 'Lord! Lord! Lord!' When he had
received about twenty lashes, the driver stopped to
pull up the poor man's shirt (or rather smockfrock),
which had worked down upon his galled posteriors.
The sufferer then cried, 'Think me no man? think
me no man?' By that exclamation I understood him
to say, 'Think you I have not the feelings of a man?'
The flogging was instantly recommenced and continued; the negro continuing to cry, 'Lord! Lord!
Lord!' till thirty-nine lashes had been inflicted.
When the man rose up from the ground, I perceived
the blood oozing out from the lacerated and tumified
parts where he had been flogged, and he appeared
greatly exhausted, but he was instantly ordered off
to his usual occupation.

"Two young women of about the same age were,
one after the other, then laid down and held by four
men, their backs most indecently uncovered, and
thirty-nine lashes of the blood-stained whip inflicted
upon each poor creature's posteriors. Their exclamation, likewise, was, 'Lord! Lord! Lord!' They
seemed also to suffer acutely, and were apparently a
good deal lacerated. Another woman (the sixth

offender) was laid down and uncovered for the lash,
but at the intercession of one of the drivers she was
reprieved.

" The overseer stood by and witnessed the whole
of the cruel operation, with as much seeming indif-
ference as if he had been paying them their wages.
I was, meanwhile, perfectly unmanned by mingled
horror and pity. Yet I have no reason to believe
that the *natural* feelings of this young man (whose
age did not exceed twenty-four years) were less humane or sensitive than my own. But such is the
callousness which constant familiarity with scenes of
cruelty engenders. He had been a book-keeper for
four years previously, on another estate belonging to
the same proprietors, and had been appointed overseer on this estate only a few months before. His re-
ception of me when I arrived was so kind, frank,
and cordial, that I could not have believed him, had
I not seen it with my own eyes, to be *capable* of in-
flicting such cruelty on a fellow-creature.

" *12th instance.* — The first of these two cases was
that of a married woman, the mother of several children. She was brought up to the overseer's door
one morning, and one of the drivers who came with
her accused her of having stolen a fowl. Some
feathers, said to have been found in her hut, were
exhibited as evidence of her guilt. The overseer
asked her if she could pay for the fowl. She said
something in reply which I did not clearly understand. The question was repeated, and a similar
reply again given. The overseer then said, ' Put
her down.' On this the woman set up a shriek, and

rent the air with her cries of terror. Her countenance grew quite ghastly, and her lips became pale
and livid. I was close to her, and particularly noticed
her remarkable aspect and expression of countenance.
The overseer swore fearfully, and repeated his order,
'Put her down!' The woman was then extended on
the ground and held down by two negroes. Her gown
and shift were literally torn from her back, and, thus
brutally exposed, she was subjected to the cart-whip.
The punishment inflicted on this poor creature was
inhumanly severe. She was a woman somewhat
plump in her person, and the whip being wielded
with great vigour, every stroke cut deep into the
flesh. She writhed and twisted her body violently
under the infliction,—moaning loudly, but uttering
no exclamation in words, except once, when she cried
out entreating that her nakedness might not be indecently exposed,—appearing to suffer, from matronly
modesty, even more acutely on account of her in-
decent exposure, than the cruel laceration of her
body. But the overseer only noticed her appeal by a
brutal reply, and the flogging continued. Disgusted
as I was, I witnessed the whole to a close. I num-
bered the lashes, stroke by stroke, and counted *fifty*,
thus exceeding by eleven the number allowed by the
colonial law to be inflicted at the arbitrary will of
the master or manager. This was the only occasion
on which I saw the legal number of thirty-nine
lashes exceeded; but I never knew the overseer or
head book-keeper give less than thirty-nine. This
poor victim was shockingly lacerated. When permitted to rise she again shrieked violently. The

overseer swore roughly, and threatened, if she was
not quiet, to put her down again. He then ordered
her to be taken to the hot-house, or hospital, and put
in the stocks. She was to be continued in the stocks
for several nights, while she worked in the yard
during the day at light work. She was too severely
mangled to be able to go to the field for some days.
This flogging took place on the 27th of September."

Nor could these sickening severities have been at
all unusual. For in the four " crown colonies," * the
home government was able to do what it pleased, and
accordingly it required every planter to give in sworn
returns of the punishments inflicted on his estate.
By these sworn returns there were registered, in the
two years 1828-9, 68,921 punishments. The law
allowed, in the crown colonies, twenty-five stripes to
a punishment, which limit was incessantly passed.
Taking the average, however, at but twenty stripes,
this puts the total amount of stripes inflicted, in
regular floggings, for these four colonies alone, in
two years, at no less than one million three hundred
and fifty thousand! Twenty-five thousand and ninety-
four punishments, or. at that rate, half a million, of
those stripes were sworn to as having been inflicted
upon *females*.†

That the whip, and the dread of the whip, must
have caused an unspeakable amount of physical and
moral misery, is then plain enough. In this respect
emancipation has beyond all question caused a vast

* Guiana (at that time divided), Trinidad, St. Lucia.
† Protector's Reports, Parl. Papers.

c

accession to human happiness, in that it has substi-
tuted the attraction of rewards for the compulsion of
terror. But by far the most portentous and striking
of the features of West Indian society under slavery
was this, that while the free negroes were steadily
advancing in number, the slaves were dying off at a
rate which was described at the time as " appalling."

It was not by stories of atrocious cruelty that the
eyes of Parliament were opened to the wickedness
and folly of slavery. If any of our readers would
turn to the pages of Hansard, they would find that
what gave the death-blow to slavery, in the minds of
English statesmen, were the population returns, which
showed the fact, " the appalling " fact, that although
only eleven out of the eighteen islands had sent them
in, yet in those eleven islands the slaves had decreased
in twelve years, by no less than 60,219 : namely, from
558,194 to 497,975 !* Had similar returns been pro-
cured from the other seven colonies (including Mauritius, Antigua, Barbadoes, and Grenada), the decrease
must have been little, if at all, less than 100,000!
Now it was plain to every one that if this were really
so, the system could not last. The driest economist
would allow that " it would not pay " to let the working classes be slaughtered. To work the labouring men
of our West Indies to death might bring in a good
return for a while, but could not be a profitable en-
terprise in the long run. Accordingly, this was the

---

* Parl. Papers, Population returns for the West Indies. They
are given in the appendix to the Life of Sir Fowell Buxton. Of
course the decrease by manumission is not included.

main — we had almost said the only — topic of the debates on slavery in 1831 and 1832. Is slavery causing a general massacre of the working-classes in our sugar islands, or is it not, was a question worth debating, in the pounds, shillings, and pence view, as well as in the moral one. And debated it was, long and fiercely. The result was the full establishment of the dreadful fact. The slaves, as Mr. Marryatt said, were " dying like rotten sheep." And the fatal influence of that mortality upon the wealth of the islands was already making itself felt. Nay, even so early as 1816, Mr. M. G. Lewis observes that

" Throughout the island many estates, formerly very flourishing and productive, have been thrown up for want of hands to cultivate them, and are now suffered to lie waste ; four in my own immediate neighbourhood are in this situation. Finding their complement of negroes de-crease, and having no means of recruiting them, proprietors of two estates have in numerous instances found themselves obliged to give up one of them, and draw off the negroes for the purpose of properly cultivating the other."*

Whatever then may be said for West Indian slavery, this damning thing must be said against it, that *the slaves were dying of it*. Then came emancipation. The tide at once turned. In the next twelve years,

* The same melancholy truth holds good of *slaves employed in field labour* everywhere. In Cuba it is an ascertained fact that the average life of the prædial slaves is only seven or eight years! Hence their great need of the slave trade. Nor could those of the United States, which produce sugar, maintain the number of their slaves, if they were not fed by a great internal slave trade from the breeding states.

there was an *increase* of 54,076 in the number of the
negroes of but ten colonies (no return having been
sent from the larger ones), and since then the population of the West Indies has been increasing steadily.
This one fact is enough by itself to justify emancipation. Whatever evils might have sprung from that
act, nothing could be so bad for both master and men
as to have all the latter killed off. Yet such was the
limit towards which things were actually tending,
and that swiftly. Had the same rate of decrease gone
on, one century would have seen the extinction of
slavery, by the extinction of the slaves. We put it
to the good sense of our readers, whether it would
have answered to let this state of things proceed.

We have shown, then, how deep and how murderous was the wretchedness into which the working
class of the West Indies was thrust by slavery. We
have given some glimpses of the oppression they en-
dured, and how they perished under it. So far, then,
as the mass of the people went, it plainly was not
only a good but a wise thing to cut their bonds.
And, perhaps, now-a-days, it may seem strange that
it should ever have been wished to keep such a state
of things going, for the sake of a small body of gentlemen. But what made the matter wholly unbear-
able was, that it had not even the poor merit of
enriching those for whose good the system was held
to. Never did the truth come out with greater clearness than in the West Indies, that it is short-sighted
folly to thrust aside natural arrangements, and set up
artificial ones in their stead. Here was a body of
men owning some of the richest land in the world.
They had plenty of labourers, and might lash as much

work out of them as they pleased. They had a tight
monopoly, so tight that not even the sugar of England's other dominions of India or Singapore was
allowed to compete. Yet, despite all this, even from
the beginning of the century, the planters were continually laying before the Colonial Secretary and
Parliament, memorials which might truly be said to
have been " written within and without, with lamen-
tation and mourning and woe." *

If we reproduced these now stale and forgotten
complaints of the planters, they would seem worse
bores than Cowper's friend, who

> " thought he should have died, he was so bad :
> His peevish hearers almost wished he had."

We will only therefore show what the pecuniary
condition of the planters was in 1830, when slavery
and monopoly were at their zenith. Nor let it be
said that their deep distress was owing to the anti-
slavery agitation. They do not so much as allude
to it.

Lord Chandos †, in 1830, presented a petition from
the West India merchants and planters setting forth
" the extreme distress under which they labour ; "
and he declared in his speech that it was " not possible for them to bear up against such a pressure
any longer." . . . " They are reduced to a state

---

* See (for a brief analysis of these) Sir H. Barkly's Report,
1854. In the twenty years ending with 1792 (according to a
report of the Jamaica House of Assembly), there were lodged
with the provost marshal of that island no less than 80,121 exe-
cutions, to the amount of 22,568,786*l.* !

† The debate is given in the "West India Reporter," 1830.

in which they are obliged earnestly to solicit relief
from Parliament." Mr. Bright said, "The distress
of the West India colonial body is unparalleled in
the country. Many families who formerly lived in
comparative affluence are reduced to absolute penury."
The "West India Reporter" also quotes a report on
the commercial state of the West Indies, which said,
" There are the strongest concurrent testimonies and
proofs that unless some speedy and efficient measures
of relief are adopted, the ruin of a great number of
the planters must inevitably very soon take place."

Again, the Committee of 1832 reported that they
had received abundant evidence of the distress of the
planters, "which is said to have existed in a considerable degree for ten or twelve years past, and to
have been greatly aggravated within the last three
or four." They state that the immediate cause of
distress is " the inadequacy of return." The receipts
of the planter did not cover his outlay ; and not only
so, but production was decreasing as well. Thus in
the five years ending with 1820, the export of sugar
from Jamaica had been 585,172 hogsheads ; but had
fallen to 493,784 in the five years ending with 1830,
a decrease of no less than 91,388 hogsheads. Nay, in
the ten years ending with 1830, the decrease was no
less than 201,843 hogsheads from the amount in the
ten years ending with 1830.*

*   1,196,072
               994,229
               ————————
               201,843 hogsheads.

See table of exports from Jamaica, in the appendix to Bigelow's
" Jamaica."

And here is a fact which plainly shows that these distresses would only have grown deeper and heavier had slavery been allowed to go on. In the Dutch colony of Surinam, the very same ruin has come on which befell our own islands. The fact that slavery was left standing has made not the least difference. " Out of 917 plantations in that colony, 636 *have been totally abandoned!* " Mark that! Here we have a large colony, with slavery preserved in all its force and beauty. And what is the result? The result is almost total ruin. " Out of 917 plantations, 636 have been totally abandoned! " " Of the remainder, 65 grow nothing but wood or provisions." And the small balance are stated to be on the road to destruction.

The state of things then with which the statesmen of 1833 were forced to grapple was this: — Here was a system kept going by the sheer force of the law, which allowed no rights whatever to some 800,000 serfs, which regarded them as beasts of burden, made for nothing but to enrich a few English gentlemen by their forced toil; which was slaughtering these workmen; which at the same time had brought down their owners to a state of "unparalleled" distress; had reduced these noblemen and gentlemen of England to the degrading necessity of " earnestly " begging Parliament for " relief ; " and was steadily decreasing the productive powers of these fertile islands. Such was the result of the defiance that had been hurled at the laws of nature. Massacre of the working class; ruin of the proprietors; such was the work that slavery and mo-

nopoly were doing under the sun. And this is the
state of things to which many eyes still look back
with tender regrets! Yet Carlyle himself, the chief
hater of the philanthropists, with his wonted force,
has told us, that —

"To prosper in this world, to gain felicity, victory, and
improvement, either for a man or a nation, there is but one
thing requisite, — that the man or nation can discern what
the true regulations of the universe are in regard to him
and his pursuits, and can faithfully and steadily follow these.
These will lead him to victory. Whoever it may be that
sets him in the way of these . . . . sets him in the sure
way to please the Author of this Universe, and is his
friend of friends. And, again, whoever does the contrary
is, for a like reason, his enemy of enemies. This may be
taken as fixed."

Taken as fixed it certainly may be; and fixed it
plainly was in the West Indies, where the artificial
arbitrary interference of law with the natural freedom of man, and freedom of trade, was bringing about
the extinction of the working class, and was whirling
their masters along to utter ruin.

It is not within our purpose to discuss why and
wherefore slavery and monopoly should have wrought
such unlooked-for devastation in lieu of the wealth
which they were meant to foster. But we may
notice that elsewhere, too, the same folly has been
no less fatal. The gradual decay of Italy under the
emperors has been attributed by the best authorities
in a great degree to the substitution of slave for free
labour. Russia has kept her peasants in serfdom
later than any other Christian country, and Russia is

far behind the world in all wealth, of purse as well
as mind. But most strikingly is this the case with
the Slave States of North America. Every tra-
véller of weight dwells on the poverty-stricken look
of those states, rich as their soil, genial as their
climate may be, when set beside the Free States of
the same union. Their condition has been thoroughly
investigated, and, we might almost say, photographed,
by the celebrated American agriculturist, Mr. Olmsted;
and he, applying to the matter the skilled mind of a
practical farmer, gives overwhelming proofs of the
destructive effect of slavery, and points out with great
clearness how it must be that, in the long run, it costs
less to hire a fit man for doing what has to be done,
than to maintain a whole colony of people, and force
labour out of them by the terrors of the lash. We fully
perceive, in reading his painful accounts of the misery
of the Slave States, how vast a loss must arise from
the labourer's intense and unremitting resistance to
this mode of extracting his labour, — a mode by
which, if we may say so, his laziness is stimulated to
the most energetic opposition. When a whole people
is always looking at its work, with the eager thought,
How not to do it, of course the result is that it is
not done ; and, though a sharp master may flog large
work out of his slaves, yet most of them attain a high
degree of proficiency in the art of leaving that
undone which they ought to have done.

But not only does Quashee, under this system, give
his heart and soul to spending the greatest possible
time on the least possible work, but it is a universal
complaint of all slaveholders that he grows so mind-

less, so shiftless, that agriculture and manufacturing improvements are impossible. No machinery can be entrusted to slaves. Wherever slave-labour prevails you must have the most primitive tools, you must eschew all the arts by which labour is made swifter. So heavily did this blight rest on the West Indies that even the plough (since become very common) was unknown under slavery. Amusing illustrations are given by various writers, of the tiresome and irritating effects of slavery, in making the minds of the slaves a mere blank.

" Somehow or other," says Lewis, " they never can manage to do anything *quite* as it should be done. If they correct themselves in one respect to-day, they are sure of making a blunder in some other manner to-morrow. Cubina is now twenty-five, and has all his life been employed about the stable; he goes out with my carriage twice every day; but he has never yet been able to succeed in putting on the harness properly. Before we have proceeded a hundred yards we are certain of being obliged to stop, and put something or other to rights: and I once laboured for more than half an hour to make him understand that the Christmas-holidays came at Christmas; when asked the question, he always hesitated, and answered at hap-hazard, ' July ' or ' October.' Yet Cubina is far superior in intellect to most of the negroes who have fallen under my observation. The girl too, whose business it is to open the house each morning, has in vain been desired to unclose all the jalousies : she never fails to leave three or four closed ; and when she is scolded for doing so, she takes care to open those three the next morning, and leaves three shut on the opposite side.

" Indeed, the attempt to make them correct a fault is quite fruitless : they never can do the same thing a second time in the same manner; and if the cook having succeeded in dressing a dish well is desired to dress just such another, she is certain of doing something which makes it quite different. One day I desired that there might be always a piece of salt meat at dinner, in order that I might be certain of having enough to send to the sick in the hospital. In consequence of this there was nothing at dinner but salt meat. I complained that there was not a single fresh dish, and the next day, there was nothing but fresh. Sometimes there is scarcely anything served up, and the cook seems to have forgotten the dinner altogether: she is told of it; and the next day she slaughters without mercy pigs, sheep, fowls, ducks, turkeys, and everything that she can lay her murderous hands upon, till the table absolutely groans under the load of her labours."

The inevitable tendency of slavery to make the working class so idle and shiftless is, we believe, the true reason why, in the long run, it has always been the ruin of the nation that clings to it. But, whether this be or be not the true explanation, we have seen that, as a matter of fact, the West India planters and merchants were " reduced to a state in which they were obliged earnestly to solicit relief from Parliament " — in truth, were sinking swiftly and surely into the abyss. It was not then shortsighted of the British Parliament to put an end to this wretched state of things. In truth no one now thinks that it would have been wise to leave slavery standing. But those who were displeased by emancipation are now-a-days wont not to complain of the thing itself, but of the way in which it was done. They complain bitterly that the slaves were set free in hot haste ; whereas, had steps been taken to pave

the way and soften the change, all would have been
well. This view has much truth in it. And if
emancipation has been attended with evils that might
have been escaped, the Abolitionists may fairly lay
the blame thereof on those who would not allow that
gradual preparation for the change, which they earnestly sought for. We have no wish to cast blame on
the planters. They had much to vex them, and they
have paid dearly for their lack of foresight ; but we
must notice the vast blunder they made in withstand-
ing those mitigating measures which might have gra-
dually trained the slave to work as a hired labourer
for his former owner, instead of keeping him in the
tightest bondage till the very hour of thorough freedom. But the strangest part of the affair has been
(and it is an amusing illustration of the old fable of
the wolf and the lamb) that the Anti-slavery party *
— the very men who strenuously fought for such
mitigating measures — are now abused by the very
men who withstood these measures to the death,
for not having permitted them ! Why, till the Anti-
slavery leaders found that it was utterly hopeless to
get the West Indian planters to do any one thing
towards fitting their slaves for freedom, they were
solely bent upon such preliminary measures. In
1823, Mr. Fowell Buxton, in making the first motion
for the abolition of slavery, plainly declared that —

* It would be convenient if those who in 1809 abolished the
trade in slaves between Africa and our colonies (Wilberforce,
Stephen, Clarkson, and their coadjutors), were always called the
Abolitionists : and those who did away with *slavery* in our
colonies in 1834 were called the Anti-slavery party.

" The object at which we aim is the extinction of slavery—nothing less than the extinction of slavery—in nothing less than the whole of the British dominions. Not, however, the rapid termination of that state; not the sudden emancipation of the negro. But such preparatory steps ; such measures of precaution, as by slow degrees, and in a course of years, *first fitting and qualifying the slaves for the enjoyment of freedom*, shall gently conduct us to the annihilation of slavery."

He especially urged that the young children of the slaves should be set free, and thus slavery would by degrees have died out.

Nothing could have been more temperate than these aims : and the circular letters issued to the islands by Canning, in consequence of this debate, merely "recommended" the colonial authorities to adopt some mitigating measures that might help to train the negro for freedom. The fury, the wild spirit of rebellion, which these salutary suggestions called forth, might have warned the Abolitionists how vain it was to hope that the planters would help to soften down slavery, The feelings stirred up by the bare idea of their being advised to do so, were thus expressed in Jamaica : —

" We will pray the Imperial Parliament to amend their origin, which is bribery ; to cleanse their consciences, which are corrupt ; to throw off their disguise, which is hypocrisy ; to break with their false allies, who are the saints ; and, finally, to banish from among them all the purchased rogues, who are three fourths of their number ! " *

* Jamaica Journal, June 28, 1823.

In fact, the planters met the philanthropic advances of the British public much as the captain treated those of Parson Adams, when the latter " prayed God to bestow on him a little more humanity." The captain answered with a surly look and accent, " that he hoped he did not mean to reflect upon him ; d— him, he had as much imamity as another, and if any man said he had not, he would convince him of his mistake by cutting his throat." *

One of the " mitigating measures " so gently suggested by Canning, would, it might have been thought, have been readily adopted by Englishmen in any part of the world. It was that the flogging of females should be discontinued. Clearly there was little hope of elevating the slaves when their women might be stripped and flogged at the mercy of any ruffian who had them under his charge. If the colonists would not give up this luxury of mastership, where was improvement to begin ? Yet this question was put to the vote after due discussion in each colony, and in every one it was resolved to continue this wicked and disgusting practice.

Of course at last the Anti-slavery leaders, or rather, in fact, the British public, would stand this trifling no longer, but said clearly, that since slavery could not be softened down, it should be swept away. Still the apprenticeship was a further attempt at a mitigation before freedom ; but its only result was to irritate both the quasi masters and the quasi slaves ; and as it admitted of neither the whip nor wages,

* Joseph Andrews, ch. vii.

instead of training the negroes to work hard for hire, it merely widened the breach between them and their former owners.

We have now done with the first great period in the history of the British West Indies, the period of monopoly and slave labour, and we have clearly seen that under slavery and monopoly the labourers were dying, production lessening, agriculture barbarous, trade decaying, and the proprietors themselves — English noblemen and gentlemen — imploring the aid of Parliament to save them from their state of unparalleled distress. We have further seen that not the Anti-slavery party, but those who stood against them, were to blame if due preparation was not made for the period of transition. And in turning now to that period, we may at once admit that upon the abolition of slavery there was a large falling off in the production of sugar. The negroes were little inclined to submit to any coercion ; while the planters had not learnt to treat them as free and independent labourers, who were to be enticed, not forced, to toil. We could fill hundreds of pages with descriptions of the painful and unavailing struggles of the employers to escape by hook or by crook from the dreadful necessity of treating with respect, and alluring by wages, those whom not long before they could order to be put down and flogged for the least indolence. The only effect of those struggles (but this effect they had to a very great extent), was to disgust the negroes, and drive them to seek a livelihood anywhere rather than on the sugar plantations. Very many of the planters also gave their negroes notice

to quit their cottages and grounds, under the ide
that by such a threat they would force them to worl
for less wages.   The result was to make the negroe
shift elsewhere.*

For a time then there was some confusion, an(
many planters found it a hard task to fit themselve(
and their circumstances to a state of things so new
Unhappily too, Shakspeare's remark, that " calamitie:
come not single spies, but in battalions," was but too
well exemplified in those years.   In 1843 an awful
earthquake visited the leeward group, doing frightful
devastation.   Out of 172 sugar-mills in Antigua,
117 were either levelled with the ground or split from
top to bottom.   A third of the houses in the city of
St. John were flung down, and most of the remainder
so shattered and torn as to be untenantable.   A hurricane followed ; and the traces of these two calamities
were still visible six years after.   Churches blown
down, forest-trees uprooted, houses destroyed, and
negro huts upturned, met Mr. Baird's eye even in
1849 ; and the damage done to the sugar canes was
mournful.†   But worse than this was the series of
droughts that year after year, with only two exceptions, occurred between 1840 and 1849.‡   In eight

* See a very able and full article in the Westminster Rêview,
February, 1853.   The writer comes himself, and carries his
reader with him to the conclusion, that " The diminution of
labour was the direct and immediate consequence of the mismanagement of the planters."

† See " Antiguas and the Antiguans," and Baird's West
Indies.

‡ See the tabular return from Jamaica, Appendix B. to Mr.
Bigelow's book, p. 201.

years, six of drought would have been enough to re-
duce the planters to poverty even had they had slaves
in millions.

These were terrible drawbacks, and we by no means
deny that there was a good deal of suffering among
the owners of West Indian property during those
years. But there is a general concurrence of testimony,
that after the first unsettlement, things soon began to
find their level, and, to quote the words of the Commissioners, who inquired into the state of Guiana in
1850, "every symptom of a change for the better was
apparent; cultivation was extended, and the crops
increased; the labouring population were working
more steadily, and evinced signs of speedy improvement." Slavery ceased in 1834; and apprenticeship
in 1838. It was not till 1847 that the dreadful crash
came, which has since resounded through the world.

What led to that crash was the vast fall in the price
of sugar. The calamities that began in 1847 were
aggravated by other causes. But the true explanation
of them is to be found in the pregnant and striking
fact, that West Indian sugar, which in 1840 (exclusive of duty) sold in bond at 49s., in 1848 had sunk
to 23s. 5d.—a fall of twenty-five shillings and seven-
pence out of forty-nine shillings! Or to take a wider
area, sugar in the eight years ending with 1846, had
averaged (exclusive of duty) 37s. 3d. per cwt. In
the eight following years it averaged only 24s. 6d.
per cwt.* And mark the consequence. In the first

* Parliamentary Return of tea and sugar, July, 1818. From
this Return it also appears that, during the first twenty years of
the century, sugar fetched 48s., all but double its price from

eight years the whole production of the West Indies
was just twenty million cwt.* In the second eight
years it had increased by four million cwt. and a
half. Now, had this amount sold at the previous
prices, it would have fetched fifteen millions† more
than it actually did fetch. Whereas in reality, it sold
for seven millions less than the smaller crops of the
first period had sold for. One can imagine the feelings of the planters, who had laid themselves out to
produce larger crops, and found themselves receiving
seven millions less than they had received in the preceding eight years—fifteen millions less than they
would have received, had the old prices still ruled!
Seven millions less receipt! Why that fact by itself
would be enough to account for the outcry that was
heard from the West Indies during that time of suffering. It just made the whole difference between
profit on the business, and loss on it. In falling from
37s. 3d. to 24s. 6d., not only was the profit on the
sugar swept clean away, but a dead loss ensued,
wherever a loose system of management by agents
instead of by proprietors existed, and where a heavy
interest on mortgages had to be paid. This fact, of
that heavy fall of price, is one which demands the
most emphatic notice, if we wish to understand the
reason why the West Indies passed through the valley
of the shadow of death during those years.‡

1846–55. No wonder West India property has fallen in value
since those good old times.

* Parliamentary Return, "Sugar," February, 1858.

† Accurately, 15,430,440l.

‡ This great fall in the price of cane sugar was partly due, of

That so great a fall in the value of the one staple which the West Indies produced, would have caused grievous suffering in any society, however wholesome its condition might have been, it is easy to imagine. But what rendered the blow so deadly, was this, that the owners of West Indian property had inherited from the times of slavery and monopoly, a state of affairs in the last degree ruinous and rotten — so ruinous, so rotten, that a collapse, as Mr. Bigelow justly observes, was inevitable, whatever had been done or left undone. Whether slavery stood or not, whether monopoly stood or not, things had got to that pass when a hurricane was absolutely necessary to sweep the old order away, and make it give place to a new one. We will briefly touch on some of the traits of that old order, traits which strikingly remind us of Ireland, ere she too had been saved by her great calamity.

I. The planters were overwhelmed with debt. For instance, in the small island of St. Lucia, an Encumbered Estate Court was established in 1833, and small as the island is, in the first eighteen months, liabilities were recorded to the enormous amount of 1,089,965*l.*, all debts incurred under slavery. The number of estates disposed of by judicial sale between 1833, when the St. Lucia Encumbered Estates Act came

course, to the Free-trade measure of 1846; but also was partly due to the Protective measures, at about that time, adopted by France and Belgium, and other continental countries, in favour of their beet sugar, against cane sugar, and which caused the latter to be poured into England, instead of being diffused through Europe.

into operation, and 1844, was 76,—there being but
101 estates in the island! And the consequence has
been, that despite several heavy disadvantages —
" an insufficient population, a lack of capital; much
waste land; and plentiful and cheap food,"—all
tending to lessen the supply of labour, the production
of sugar, which in the three last years of slavery
amounted to 151,925 cwt., in the three years ending
with 1857, amounted to 193,208 cwt., being an
increase of 41,283 cwt. And as Colonel Torrens
remarks, " In few islands, perhaps, has the experiment of free labour been more successful." Here
then we have every inducement to the labourer to
withdraw from sugar cultivation, and get much more
sugar produced than under slavery, just because the
estates were not encumbered with debt.

Nor did that island stand alone. In each one of
them the same state of things prevailed. Nearly the
whole of the estates were mortgaged, many of them
far beyond their actual value; and it was almost impossible for their owners to pay a heavy interest, and
get a clear profit from the complex and precarious
business which they were vainly attempting to conduct. The system upon which the cultivation of
sugar was carried on was this : the prodigious capital
that was necessary for the purpose was annually furnished as a loan by West India merchants in London,
— the crop being then consigned to the lenders, and
sold by them in England. Of course they repaid
themselves in the first instance; but it too often happened that owing to various causes, amongst which
droughts were the most frequent and fatal, the crop

fell so short, that the advances of the merchants could not be repaid, and thus the West India proprietor became deeply indebted to them, and the heavy interest on the outstanding balances was so much dead weight on his property.

Mr. Bigelow (an American traveller of great intelligence and observation), after a diligent inquiry into this point, declares that at the time of emancipation " the island of Jamaica was utterly insolvent . . . . . nearly every estate was mortgaged for more than it was worth, and was liable for more interest than it could possibly pay . . . . . Bankruptcy was inevitable." He says again : " I have given my reasons for believing that the Emancipation Act *did not cause,* but only *precipitated,* a result which was inevitable. It compelled a balance to be struck between the debtors and creditors, which revealed, rather than begat, the poverty, which now no effort can conceal."*

II. But far the worst feature in the position of the old proprietors was this, that scarcely any of them were residents; or if they were, they had not been trained to the management of their estates. Nearly the whole of the sugar estates were owned by absentees, the greater number of whom had never set foot in the islands. Now it would be foolish to blame those who had inherited West India property for not living on their estates, to the probable destruction of their happiness and their health. Nor indeed did it follow that an English gentleman who had not been brought up to the work would have been a first-

* Bigelow's Jamaica, p. 415.

rate manager. Skill and energy were no less needed
than a strong personal interest in the result; and most
proprietors could only have furnished the last quali-
fication. Still the fact stood thus: that by far the
greater part of the West India property was not in
the hands of those whose incomes depended on its
good management; but the cultivation of the soil, and
the manufacture of its products into sugar, were both
conducted by gentlemen living in London, through
paid subordinates, who had not the least smattering
of interest in the lasting prosperity of the estate.

Now every one knows how rare it is to make a
common English farm pay, when not let, but merely
looked after by a salaried bailiff. And besides these
agricultural risks, there was in the planter's case the
whole process of manufacture to be conducted, in-
volving a frightful outlay and requiring nice care.
All this was to be done by the proprietor's agent.
Now in not a few cases the agent was an honest man,
in spite of his great temptations ; a sober man, in
spite of the abundance of rum and the practices of
West Indian society ; an energetic man, in spite of
the enervating climate ; and also a skilful man in the
conduct of these large interests. But oftener, he was
merely an attorney, who lived in Jamaica for the ex-
press purpose of getting all the plunder he could : he
was much fonder of his bottle and his brown girl, or
girls, than of his duty ; his vigour had been perspired
away, or had disappeared under repeated attacks of
fever, ague, and delirium tremens ; he knew little of
the sound methods of management; and he had several
properties to attend to, and often one of his own,

which of course took precedence of other people's.
As an illustration of the last common occurrence, we
may mention that a memorial to Sir Henry Barkly*
was signed by eleven gentlemen, "staple producing
residents;" and they expressly state that they—these
eleven men—are either owners or agents for one hundred and twenty-three estates!† Fancy eleven men
managing the agriculture and manufacture of sugar
upon one hundred and twenty-three estates, under a
tropical sun. In Montserrat again, Dr. Davy tells us,
that out of thirty-nine estates four only were in the
hands of resident proprietors; and *twenty-three* of the
rest were managed by one and the same agent! No
wonder that nineteen of them were reputed to be
"imperfectly cultivated" or "abandoned." In St.
Kitt's there were one hundred and forty-three estates,
and eight resident owners!‡ Mr. Bigelow fell in
with a gentleman who had come over to make out for
himself why he was always sinking more and more
money on his estate. He found that his agent lived
sixty miles away, and was obliged to make the morti-
fying confession that he had never once seen it! But
in truth the proprietors were forced to put up with
what they could get, for it was no easy matter to find
an Englishman who knew anything at all about sugar
plantations, and who would go out to swelter away
his life in Jamaica. There is no reason to blame the
landlords for being absentees. There is no reason to

* In 1852.
† "Return, Sugar-growing Colonies, Jamaica," p. 141.
‡ Dr. Davy, "West Indies," p. 459.

blame them for employing the only agents they could
find.   But that this system was sure in due time to
end in bankruptcy and ruin seemed clear.

Mr. Bigelow attributes the calamities that have be-
fallen Jamaica almost wholly to this cause.   He
stoutly affirms that, even had slavery and monopoly
been preserved, still the island must have been drag-
ged down by other causes to poverty and ruin, and in
the front rank of those causes he places the absenteeism of the landlords.   After a minute examination
of the disastrous effects of the absenteeism in the
management of the estate, he says, —

"I scarcely conversed with any man of substance in
Jamaica on this subject, who had not some story to tell me
of the carelessness, improvidence, and corruption of these
middlemen. . . . . It is a common thing, I was told, for
the overseers to keep down the returns, and to increase the
expenses of estates . . . . until the owner . . . . should
send out authority to sell it for what it will bring.   These
overseers would then buy it in themselves at a ruinous
sacrifice."   "For my own part, I can see no one aspect in
which absenteeism is not a calamity to the colonies, nor do
I think it easy to ascribe to it too large a proportion of
these present distresses. "

III. That an absentee landlord, deep in debt,
plundered, deceived, and his interest neglected by
his agent, was in a very precarious position, even
while sugar was selling for a splendid price, will
readily be allowed.   What then was his inevitable
fate when sugar sank from 49s., in 1840, to 23s. 5d.
in 1848 !

The reader will naturally think that the planter

was ruined, because, not only must his profits have
been swept away, but he must have been producing
at a great loss.   That was true.   But that was not
the real thing that brought the West Indies to such
a crash.   What struck society there to the heart was
not the mere loss of profit, nor the mere loss of the
year's transactions, but that hence arose a total loss
of credit, and without credit, *there was an end of the
supply of capital.*

One of the main features in the conduct of West
India affairs had been this — that the vast capital
requisite for the production of the sugar crops (a
capital of not less than some millions) had been
annually advanced by the West Indian merchants
in London, on the security of the crops, which
were then consigned to them.   But, of course, when
it was known that sugar had fallen so enormously in
value, the merchants took fright — the credit of the
planter was gone.   He was embarked in transactions
on which a vast capital had been already laid out,
and which required a vast capital to carry them on,
and *capital he could not obtain!*   Every other circumstance in the state of the West Indies — the in-
debtedness of the planters, their absenteeism, the
lack of labourers, and so forth, may, more or less,
have aggravated their difficulties, but here lay the
very gist, here lay the very soul of the matter;
that suddenly the agriculturists and manufacturers of
these islands (for such the planters were) found themselves bereft of capital.

And what added to the dreadful pinch for means,
to the impossibility of procuring it on almost any

terms, was that at this very period the great crisis of 1847 fell on the commercial world; and, as though the West Indians were to drink the cup of destruction to the dregs, the West Indian Bank failed for a vast sum.

Such, then, was the state of things when the competition of Cuba and Brazil was let in upon the planters. Deep in debt; absentees; dependent on loans for their supplies of capital, never did a great change fall on men so little prepared. And the results were terrible. The reader would hardly thank us if we described them. Nor does it lie within our province to do so. All we have wished has been to point out how unjustly these events have been charged upon emancipation, when they were clearly due to the great fall in the price of sugar, and the collateral circumstances which we have described. In fact, although the less informed British public has carelessly assumed that it was emancipation, and not these other incidents, which led to the ruin of the West Indies, this seems to be scarcely ever the opinion of the colonial writers themselves.

Thus the Commissioners who inquired into the state of Guiana, in 1850, expressly affirm that —

" The cause of the present depressed condition of British Guiana is, in the solemn and deliberate opinion of your Commissioners, as already expressed, *mainly* attributable to the fatal operation of the Sugar Act of 1846. Every symptom of a change for the better was apparent until then; the cultivation had been extended and the crops increased; the labouring population were working more steadily, and evinced signs of speedy improvement. That

destructive measure, coupled with the want of early and
sufficient immigration, inflicted a blow from which this
colony has never recovered. Everything has retrograded
from that moment, a great number of estates have been
abandoned, and with the decline of the agricultural interest,
the condition of the lower orders has very sensibly deteri-
orated."

They afterwards allude " to the fatal Sugar Act,"
and state that it was that Act which at once pros-
trated the whole landed interest of the country.

We have the authority of the Attorney-General of
Trinidad for the fact, that in two years after the
Act of 1846, nearly all the mercantile houses con-
nected with the colony had been struck down ; sixty-
four petitions of insolvency filed ; and estate after
estate thrown upon the market, and no purchaser
found. " No hurricane in its terrible consequences,"
says a Jamaica writer, "was ever so disastrous to
the colony as the Act of 1846. To that alone we
may trace the rapid downfall of Jamaica." * And
thus Mr. Bigelow, in speaking of the politicians of
Jamaica, tells us that —

"It is to free trade they ascribe their ruin, not to the
abolition of slavery. I did not find a man upon the island
—and I made very extensive inquiry—who regretted the
Emancipation Act, or who, if I may take their own pro-
fessions, would have restored slavery had it been in their
power."

In Lord Stanley's second letter†, it is stated by a

* Quoted in the " West India Labour Question," p. 8.
† Lord Stanley's " State of the West Indies," p. 52.

correspondent that "according to a Report of a Committee of the House of Assembly, 140 sugar and 165 coffee estates, named in that report, were abandoned since the passing of the Act of Emancipation; but, in point of fact, *nearly all these properties have been broken up since the alteration of the Coffee Duties in* 1844, *and the Sugar Duties in* 1846." And it is very remarkable that in Barbadoes, where the population is, if anything, too large; where "labour was abundant," at "from 5*d.* to 8*d.* a day,"* even there Lord Stanley tells us that a change of hands took place "*at the expense and ruin of the former owners,* from whom their properties passed at a greatly diminished value." * We will only add an observation of Dr. Davy's, who says that —

" So long as the market prices were remunerative, and the favouring circumstances unchanged, the system of high and speculative agriculture appeared to proceed prosperously. Wages were high, trade brisk, a great activity prevailed. But when prices fell, as they did in a remarkable manner on the admission of slave-grown sugar into the English market, all this apparent prosperity was at an end; disaster followed on disaster, insolvencies, scarcity of the circulating medium, suspension of credit, reduction of wages, suspension of cash payments, with threatened scarcity even of the necessaries of life. The whole, such as was witnessed in 1847-48, was a concatenation of events as distressing as instructive, and affording a lesson which should, though it is doubtful that it will, be long remembered. Since then the tendency has been to return to the old plan ; and what is remarkable, and very creditable to

* Lord Stanley's " State of the West Indies," part II. pp. 35, 36.

the energies of the planters, whilst more provisions have
been grown, the culture of the cane has also increased." *

But now mark this. The old planting interest fell,
and great was the fall of it. But although the lower
prices crushed those who were overwhelmed with
debt, and who were managing the agricultural and
manufacturing processes from London by agents, still
free trade did not for one moment hinder the production of sugar.

Since 1840, the importation of sugar to the United
Kingdom from the West Indies has gone forward as
follows : —

		cwt.
Six years before free trade (1841-6)	. .	14,629,550
Six years after free trade (1847-52)	. .	17,918,362
Last six years . . . . (1853-8)	. .	18,443,331.

It will be seen that these amounts are progressive.†
And so, too, if, instead of six, we take the eight years
that followed free trade, there was an increase of
production, to the large amount of 4,535,882 cwt.
upon the previous eight years. This is a point of
the very highest importance, as regards the question

---

* Dr. Davy's " West Indies," p. 128.

† We have taken the returns from the Sugar Return of 1858.
But from the custom-house returns of Jamaica, it would seem
that a far larger export took place than that which is accounted
for by the English custom-house. Thus, in the three years
1850—1852, the English return gives 1,714,109 cwt. as imported
from Jamaica : the Jamaica return gives, as exported to Great
Britain, in those three years, 1,972,274 cwt. ; a discrepancy
of 258,165 cwt. ! The Jamaica returns are given in the return
" Sugar-Growing Colonies, 1852."

before us. It absolutely, inevitably, irresistibly demonstrates two things: first, it demonstrates that
although the old proprietors could not make the production of sugar pay, *others could.* Clearly sugar
could not have gone on steadily and rapidly increasing
in amount unless the producers of it found it answer.
But then, secondly, it follows that the old proprietors
were ruined owing to their peculiar position,—owing
to their debts, absenteeism, and so forth; and that
it is not the lack of labourers that has been their
destruction, for with that lack the new proprietors
have had to struggle no less than the old ones.
Labour cannot have been so scarce and so costly,
that "no conceivable opulence of cane crop could
cover it,"* or clearly the cane crops would have
ceased to be grown, instead of largely increasing.

We affirm, then, that the West India crash of
1847 arose from the fall in the price in sugar, which
came upon a state of affairs rotten to the core. But
still the question is to be weighed, whether that fall
in price, and that rotten state of affairs, would have
ended in such a ruin, had slavery been still main-
tained? Was not emancipation to blame for these
miseries? for if the planters had enjoyed the full use
of the slaves' labour, would they not have tided over
those obstacles, and floated off again merrily? Had
not there been a scarcity of labour, would not those
other storms have blown in vain?

What! when the planters in the very zenith of
slavery, and sugar at its highest, were yet in a state

---

* Carlyle's Occasional Discourses.

of "unparalleled distress;" when they were driven
"earnestly to seek relief from Parliament;" can we
for one moment suppose that they could have stood
such a blow?   It would be mere folly to fancy it.
The crash would have rung through the world, as it
rang through it in 1847.   The planters would have
been ground to powder.

Now let us not be misunderstood.   We freely own
that there has been a scarcity of labour.   We freely
own that the difficulties of the planters have been
aggravated thereby.   But after long and anxious
inquiry, we have come decidedly to the conclusion,
that the crash of 1847 was *not* caused by the want of
labourers; that the want of labourers has been
troublesome, has in some cases been a severe grievance: but that this has not been the ruin of the
West Indies: that the West Indies were ruined by
the other causes we have already dilated upon: and
that *the lack of labour has been mainly due to the lack
of capital.*   Had the planters possessed the capital
requisite for the punctual payment of wages, in their
great and costly transactions, there would not have
been any grievous lack of labour.   To this question
we now turn.

At the outset, we must not forget that it was impossible but that a certain amount of labour would be
turned aside from the production of sugar, when the
slaves were set free.   Why, at once, under slavery,
women and men were worked in gangs together; and
nearly as much field labour was forced from the one
sex as from the other; the children, meanwhile, being
kept in a kind of hospital, under a nurse, while the

mothers were so engaged. Happily this system went
out with slavery. Most mothers now stay at home
to look after their homes and households. To us
this seems a clear gain, though the French Commissioners speak of it as "un malheur de position auquel
il est impossible de remédier." *   And certainly it
sliced off at once a full third of the available amount
of labour. Then, again, under slavery it, of course,
paid best to set all the slaves to the same work,
where one driver could keep an eye to them, and
their industry could be measured. But it was a far
more wholesome and profitable state of things, when
one man could choose one kind of work, and one
another, and a great variety of employment took the
place of that monotony. It was very fair, too, that
where the agent had been inhuman, his slaves, when
free, should leave him in the lurch, and refuse to
handle the hoe, with which their associations were
disgusting. And, finally, the demand for the produce
of provision grounds increased enormously, because
under slavery, the negroes had been fed to a great
extent on salt fish ; under freedom, they chose to
have fresh eatables. For all these reasons, it was at
once both inevitable and desirable that the one work
of sugar-making should absorb less, and other occupations should absorb more labour, than they had
done before. Under slavery the great host of labourers
were driven daily to one kind of task. Under freedom, every man has chosen the task that suited and
paid him best. If the result is less sugar, that is not
the least indication that the West Indies are ruined,

* Rapport de 1843, p. 23.

though it may have ruined those who had laid out a
vast capital on the manufacture of that one article.

It is further true, that in certain localities, especially on the banks of the rivers in Guiana, where the
negroes have been cut off from communication with
civilised life, and have been able to obtain a plentiful
subsistence by hunting and fishing, they have lapsed
into a state of useless barbarism.   It is also true
that in the seaports a number of filthy idlers are to
be found, who impress the casual visitor very unfa-
vourably.   The traveller, perhaps, on landing, will
offer a shilling to a sooty gentleman in rags to carry
his portmanteau ;   and the sooty gentleman thanks
massa, but " it doesn't not suit him " to take the job.
Thinking this fellow mad, he offers the chance to
another, who, after long consideration, says he will
" do anything to oblige massa."   He " hopes de Lord
will bless massa and all his family," and that " massa
will soon find a person to do what he wants ;" but he
himself is going to attend a funeral in the evening,
and " foller his parted broder to de grabe."   Of course,
the fretted traveller jumps to the conclusion that all
niggers are idle impracticable scoundrels, and, on his
return home, writes a fierce tirade against them and
the philanthropists.

But what is said by those who really know the
country ?   We have taken the Governor's Reports
for the year 1852, 1853, and 1857 *, and have searched
for information under this head.   And we confess to

* The intervening ones are not to be had at the Parl. Paper
Office.

have felt some surprise in finding that this topic, of
the scarcity of labour, is not so much as touched upon
at all, by the Governors of seven of the West Indies.
Eight of them in that long period do make some
reference to the alleged want of labour. But five of
them refer to it *to deny the fact!* The Governor of
Antigua writes, " Nor can labour be said, wherever it
is adequately and punctually remunerated, to be deficient." * The Governor of St. Vincent : —

" I do not believe that any symptoms of aversion to field
labour are now to be observed, and feel nearly confident
that, wherever proper relations subsist between the employers and those in authority under them, and the labourers, there is little difficulty in procuring people to
work, and in retaining them as long as required. No
doubt the quantity of work done is frequently unsatisfac-
tory. A labourer of any race is, perhaps, not able to work
hard from morning till night, as is done in a temperate
climate, but he may do more than is often done here without distressing himself."

The Governor of Tobago states, in 1853, that "it
cannot be said that any want of labour is experienced." And, in 1857, he adds some remarks worth
perusal:—

" The fact that a great majority of the negro population
— whether plantation labourers or otherwise — have, since
emancipation, left the plantation negro-houses, and ac-
quired comfortable residences of their own elsewhere, may
be taken as *primâ facie* evidence that they are industrious
and saving. No man contented with the mere necessities

* Report, 1853, p. 95.

of life will work, and save up money to buy a piece of land
and erect a house, and pay the taxes to which he thereby
subjects himself. I have been upwards of twenty years in
Tobago, and I deny that its peasantry are abandoned to
slothful habits. I assert, on the contrary, that a more industrious class does not exist in this world,—at least when
working for themselves. I see no reason, either, for employers on estates to find fault. In the face of our taxation,
' 8*d.*' a day is not a very remunerative wage to labourers
whose employers in Great Britain are comparatively un-
taxed for the produce which they extract from Tobago.
Better wages would procure an increase of work. A minimum of wages naturally purchases a minimum in return,
and prompts the peasantry to labour for themselves rather
than for their employers."

The Governor of St. Lucia:—

" Complaints of want of sufficient labourers have reached
me from time to time, but I have reason to think that with
the exception of two or three estates, in unfavourable localities, *there is no actual want of labour where the labourers
are paid with regularity.* This, I regret to say, is not
always the case." *

And in this very island the French Commissioners
found, " qu'on obtenait facilement le travail, à la condition de solder exactement les travailleurs chaque
samedi." †

And again in Dominica:—

"Labour not abundant except near Roseau. On the

* Rep. 1853, p. 88. At a later period, however, the cutting
of logwood seems, "by the high price that article fetched in the
market," to have "induced a large number of the more robust
labourers to abandon the steady cultivation of the cane."

† Scute des Rapp. p. 21.

windward side of the island it is on *some* estates scarce.*
The proprietors generally appear satisfied with the amount
of labour at their command." †

So much for twelve out of the fifteen West Indies.
There remain Grenada, St. Kitts, and Jamaica. In
Grenada, in 1851, " The want of labour was severely
felt."‡ Mark this, however, that the exports and
imports had increased from 205,000*l.* in 1849, to
293,000*l.* in 1851 (an increase of 88,000*l.* in two
years), which confirms the Governor's remark, that
" there seems to be a substitution rather than a ces-
sation of industry." In St. Kitts, it is complained
that "even 8*d.* for a task of four hours will not
secure continuous labour." But in spite of this the
amount of sugar produced is actually greater than in
the time of slavery!§

It seems then that, during the period intervening
between 1851 and 1858, those fourteen out of the fifteen
West Indies were not suffering from any ruinous
scarcity of labour. When the Governors of seven
do not allude to the subject ; when the Governors of
five allude to it, to give it their denial; when the
Governors of two others do refer to it, and in some
degree endorse the complaint, but still trade and
agriculture are advancing with rapid strides; why
we can but smile at those who threaten Quashee, that
" if he will not help in bringing out the spices, he
shall get himself made a slave again, and, with bene-

* Rep. 1852.   † Ibid. 1853.   ‡ Ibid. 1852.
§ Last three years of slavery, 19,825 cwt.
        „   „   before report, 22,303 cwt. (Rep. 1857, p. 192.)

ficent whip, since other methods avail not, shall be compelled to work."*

It only remains then to notice the case of Jamaica, where the difficulties of the planters have been loudly referred to the indolence of the negroes. On this subject Sir George Grey shall speak for himself.

"It is unjust to make a general imputation against the negroes of idleness; for although, in common with the inhabitants of all warm climates, they feel more than those of cold ones a liking for repose, and a sense of enjoyment in it, there are few races of men who will work harder or more perseveringly when they are sure of getting for themselves the whole produce of their labour. It is quite true, however, that they regard it as fair, and almost meritorious, to get as much as possible from their employers, and to do as little as possible for them in return. Nothing will keep them to the journeywork of their masters, if the cultivation of their own grounds or, indeed, their private interest of any sort, draw them away." †

In 1857, with the view of obtaining knowledge of the condition and prospects of those islands, a series of queries were addressed by the Anti-slavery Society to various trustworthy and respectable persons in the West Indies, the first of which is as follows:—

"Is there any real want of labour in your colony? And, if so, to what extent? And to what general causes is it to be ascribed?"

The replies to this query are, from Jamaica, that "Wherever wages are duly and properly paid, and the labourers kindly treated, I have never known of any

* Carlyle's Occasional Discourses, p. 22.
† Rep. 1852, p. 30.

E 3

want of hands." Another writer, however, says that,
" There are planters who make no complaint on the
subject: many others have not stated the whole truth;
that the irregularity and uncertainty of their payments have been the chief cause of the want, to *them*,
of labour." Another : " There can be little doubt that
a real want of labour is experienced in the colony by
proprietors of estates generally, although there, no
doubt, is an exception to the rule in certain districts."
Another: " No planter here, in Manchester, has the
least difficulty in getting his crop gathered in, and
some I know of have been obliged to refuse applica-
tions for labour." Another: " To this query, as regards the district in which I reside, I can answer
unhesitatingly in the negative. The largest proprietor has more than once assured me that he can
get as much labour as he requires: but then he makes
it a rule to discharge any overseer who neglects to
pay the labourers every Friday evening." Another:
" I have made extensive inquiries of trustworthy
persons residing in nearly all parts of the island, but
cannot ascertain that there is anywhere a deficiency
of labour: in fact, in most places there seems to be
a superabundant supply." Another : " I have no
doubt there may be some localities in which there
may be a want of agricultural labourers, but I cannot
tell where they are, certainly not in St. Ann's, Trelawney, or St. James's." Another: " I have made
diligent inquiries, personally and by correspondence,
of gentlemen of character and influence residing in
various parts of the island, but cannot learn that
there is anywhere a poverty of labour. As regards

this neighbourhood, so far from there being any want
of labour, the supply exceeds the demand." Another:
" On this point you will find a great diversity of
opinion. . . . In my own district, the labour supply
is *at times* precarious." Another : " I do not think
there is *any want*, but if there is, an advance of 20
per cent on any kind of labour would , induce the
people to leave their own work and labour on the
estates. . . . If labour is deficient, there is generally
some special reason for it : less wages than on neighbouring estates ; unkind treatment and coarse language, &c." Another : " I do not believe that there
is any real want of labour in this colony. . . . During
the last twelve months I have made extensive inquiries on the subject from labourers, merchants, and
planters, and have been invariably told that labour is
abundant." Another states that, " At the season for
planting provisions there is, no doubt, a poverty of
labour in some localities." This writer complains
that one of the difficulties in sugar cultivation that is
most serious in its effects, is the unpunctuality and
irregularity with which wages are paid. "Let these
things be removed, and I am certain there will be no
want of labour in any part of this island." Another :
" The alleged want of labour does not exist in the
parish of Hanover " (his parish). . . . " I have heard
over and over again the general cry *Labour is needed*,
but I failed to find the man that needed it. Every
one says, ' It is not that I needed it. I have as much
labour as I require.' "

Sir H. Barkly, again, refers, in 1856, to the " large
body of labourers who had gone to work on the

Panama Railway, and elsewhere on the Spanish main." This circumstance is thus alluded to in the " West India Labour Question:"—

"I know many labourers," writes a gentleman from May Hill, Jamaica, Feb. 1857, " who, because the demand for labour is so irregular, and because the value of labour is so low, prefer renting land at 20s. per acre, and raising provisions for the market, whose labour would be available were there a steady demand and adequate remuneration for it. Why, much as our people dislike the ocean, they went in scores from Jamaica to the isthmus to labour on the railroad, when a tempting wage was within their reach."

That the negro can make more by cultivating his provision ground, than by working for hire at five or six shillings a week, is not surprising. It is stated by Lord Harris that in Trinidad a negro can make 10l. per acre by the cultivation of provision grounds.* If that is so, it shows that more wealth is extracted from the ground in that way than in the production of the old staples. And unluckily the legislation adopted in Jamaica, and some of the other islands, with the view of driving the negro from the cultivation of his own ground, has had precisely the opposite effect. Strangely enough, with that end in view, a very heavy import duty has been placed on provisions, —no less at one time than 46 per cent on beef and pork, 40 per cent on herrings, and 25 per cent on flour. The result has been, as might have been fore-

* Return, 1853, p. 157. In Barbadoes the negroes pay rent of 7l. per acre for their provision grounds. (Sharpe's Evidence before Committee, 1842.)

seen, that these duties, making it bad to buy and good to sell, were, as Lord Grey states in one of his despatches, "directly calculated to discourage the labourer from working for hire, and to lead him to prefer working on his own provision ground."

Dr. Davy, who merely records the conclusions he has come to as an impartial scientific observer, denies altogether the indolence of the negroes. "As labourers," he says, "both the women and men are allowed to be efficient, and with ordinary motives to exertion, such as fair wages *justly and regularly paid,* and liberal treatment, not wanting in industry. It is a mistake often committed to suppose that the African is by nature idle and indolent, less inclined to work than the European. It is a mistake, I perceive, even fallen into by some of the friends of the race." After quoting a remark to that effect of the Bishop of Oxford, he proceeds. "This, I have no hesitation in remarking, is a mistake founded on ignorance;" and he gives a long series of examples of the hard work done by ordinary negro labourers. "He who has witnessed, as I have, their indefatigable and provident industry, will be disposed probably to overrate rather than underrate the activity of the negro, and his love of, or rather I would say, his non-aversion to, labour."* The testimony of so independent and acute an observer as Dr. Davy, to the "indefatigable and provident industry of the negro," is remarkable.

---

* West Indies, p. 91. Dr. Davy's book is mainly extremely scientific, as might have been expected from a brother of Sir Humphry Davy.

We will only add the high authority of Sir Joshua
Rowe, Chief Justice of Jamaica, who at a public
meeting, in 1850, said, "that he had heard a great
deal, and read a great deal, of the scarcity of labour,
but from all his experience he was inclined to the
belief that the scarcity was purely local. He had
found frequently that while one estate was provided
with abundant labour, a neighbouring estate could
not procure a single labourer," owing to the manager's
fault. And what confirms this view is, that labour,
which some say is so hard to get, is wasted by the
employers in the most careless way. From the hoe
being still used on many estates, instead of the horse-
plough, twelve or fifteen labourers do what one man
could if aided by the latter implement!* Mr. Bigelow ridicules the West Indians for complaining of the
want of labour, while as an illustration of the way it
is wasted he mentions his finding three men and two
boys set to watch one herd of seventy-five cattle!
Dr. Davy also dwells on the same point, and describes
" seeing a party of labourers, highly paid, employed
in repairing a breach in a sea embankment, carrying
clay on their heads in small baskets, and trudging
through the adhesive clay, — barefooted of course;
where labourers in this country would be working
and walking easily, using wheelbarrows for carrying,
and planks for walking on."

The mass of facts and evidence we have adduced
seems to prove that, although inevitably a certain

* See Mr. Wemyss Anderson's Lecture at Kingston, on his
return from the United States.   Given by Bigelow, p. 131.

quantum of labour was withdrawn from the sugar
estates and other employments, and although in many
localities the negroes have much preferred the cultivation of their own grounds to labouring for hire, yet,
as a general rule, the facility of procuring labourers
has mainly depended on the proprietors having sufficient capital for the punctual payment of wages.
Here has been the real lack.   Here has been the
real bar to improvement.   This has been the hinge
of the matter.   In thousands of cases the proprietor
has not had the means to meet the market value of
the negroes' labour, and to pay it down on the nail
every Friday.   Labourers have been forthcoming
when the landlord has had the capital to *outbid the
provision ground*, and to pay *in cash*.   But this last
condition was at one time not possible to many
planters.   We have noticed the disastrous effect of
the Act of 1846, and of the unhappy events that
came along with it, in frightening the London merchants from making their usual advances of capital.
The lack of coin that ensued was frightful,—so frightful that in Montserrat, it is stated in the Parliamentary
Papers of 1851, some labourers actually perished of
starvation though large sums were due to them for
wages!   In 1847, seventeen sugar estates in that
island were abandoned.   On nine of them the labourers had been paid at long and uncertain intervals,
from six to twelve, and even eighteen, months. " The
large amount of 600*l.* is reported as due from one
proprietor to his people." *   In other islands the

* Davy, p. 420.

planters were driven to the expedient of endeavour-
ing to lower wages from 9*d.* to 7*d.* or even 5*d.* a day.
This was resented by the negroes. They struck
work; and finding it not worth their while to labour
on the sugar estates, they betook themselves, far more
than they had before done, to the cultivation of waste
lands. The tie between them and the estates, once
severed, could not easily be made good again. And
as in other cases of migration, every seceder exercised
an attraction upon others. Thus it happened that
at the very crisis, when everything else was going
wrong with the planter, his want of capital added to
him the further mortification of snapping the tie between him and his workmen. Being bare of cash, he
became bare of labour.

Not indeed that wages were high. Sir A. Alison,
truly, is pleased to tell us that the negroes are "so
extravagant in their demand for wages," as well as
irregular and inconsistent in their habits, "as to ren-
der it impossible to continue the cultivation of sugar
with any prospect of profit." And Carlyle, with his
usual vigour and picturesqueness, draws a portrait of
the negro, who, "sunk to the ears in pumpkin, im-
bibing saccharine juices, and much at his ease in the
creation, can listen to the less fortunate white man's
'demand,' and take his own time in supplying it.
'Higher wages, massa: higher, for you cannot wait:
still higher,'—till no conceivable opulence of cane
crop will cover such wages."*

Since neither the solemn pedant nor the eccentric

* Occasional Discourses, p. 4.

genius give any facts as to the " extravagant wages" which " no conceivable opulence of crop will cover," it might be fancied that the planter has to pay two or three times as much to his labourers as the English farmer. Now, all the official reports, the evidence before the Committee of 1841, as well as the works of travellers—in fact all authorities, concur in giving the average wages of the field negro at one shilling a day, or six shillings a week.* Six shillings a week may seem awful to a quondam slave-owner; but if it really were a rate of wages which no opulence of crop would cover, then that crop must and would be given up. Its cultivation could only be the artificial result of fiscal follies, not the one really suitable to the soil and climate.

The " impecuniosity" (to use Johnson's phrase) of the planters led to a mode of payment for labour which has been noticed by several judicious writers upon the West Indies as being unspeakably mischievous. The planters having little money, but plenty

* The stipendiary magistrates in Jamaica, in 1854, gave the following reply to the query, What is the rate of wages for able-bodied field labourers ?

> Seven say 6s. a-week.
> One says 4s. 6d.
> Two say 4s. 6d. up to 6s.
> Two ,, 4s. 6d. ,, 9s.
> One says 7s. 6d. ,, 9s.
> One ,, 9s. ,, 12s.
> One ,, 6s. ,, 12s.
> Two make no reply.

Out of the fifteen replies ten place the maximum at six shillings a week. (Parl. Papers, Jamaica, 1854.)

of rich land, were tempted to give very small wages
(4*d.* or even 2*d.* a day, according to Dr. Davy), and
then to eke out this pittance by allowing the negroes
" almost an unlimited quantity of land in lieu of
wages."*   Now, it would not even require Lord
Macaulay's schoolboy to discern, that if you pay a
man for tilling your land by giving him land of his
own, he will bestow the least possible time on your
acres, and the greatest possible time on his own. The
planter's feeling is, " I have given Quashee five rich
acres, and he is bound in exchange to give me so
much hard work." Quashee's feeling is, " What is the
good of my five rich acres, if I give all my industry to
massa, instead of to them ?" And thus a whole world
of quarrels has arisen, and the negroes have been
made irregular and idle, and the planters have been
exasperated, while the lookers-on have vainly pointed
out the folly of the whole system. In fact its folly
is so plain, that we can only explain the prevalence
of this mode of paying labour by the fact noticed
above, namely, that the planters had little money and
abundance of land, which was of no use to them, but
was of high value to the negroes *if they tilled it.*†

---

* Davy, p. 221.

† This system is continually alluded to in the Reports. In
Grenada, one of the stipendiary magistrates states that "it is
this system which has led to the ruin of numerous properties in
this island." In Jamaica, Mr. Gurney's book is filled with regrets at the general adoption of this practice. In Guiana, "the
negroes are allowed as much land as they can cultivate." In
Trinidad, "they choose as much as they can cultivate." See
also also Dr. Davy's book passim.

As regards the scarcity of labour, therefore, we believe that the state of the case was very fairly summed up by the French Commissioners who inquired into the state of the West Indies, and who, on leaving Guiana, observe:—

" A la Guyane les uns (des planteurs) proclament l'impossibilité de marcher avec le régime actuel. Les autres, au contraire, assurent qu'ils ne manquent jamais d'ouvriers, qu'ils n'ont qu'à se louer de l'assiduité des noirs, qu ils produisent autant que sous les régimes précédentes :" . . . . voilà pour les anciens planteurs. Maintenant, consultez les nouveaux : entendez ces hommes qui ne connaissent le travail forcé que par tradition : vous trouverez chez eux unanimité : tous vous diront qu'ils sont satisfaits du travail ; que leurs exploitations vont bien."

There seem, then, to be conclusive reasons for the opinion, that it was not emancipation which caused the West Indian crisis of 1847, but that the distresses of that period arose from the loss of monopoly, coming upon a most artificial and ruinous state of affairs. It seems to us indubitable that the loss of monopoly would have produced exactly the same crash, whether slavery had been standing or had been done away. And although we own that there has been in many places a scarcity of labour, and this has been a serious annoyance to the proprietors, yet we think the evidence proves that it was not so much the difficulty of obtaining labour which caused the penury of the planters, as it was the penury of the planters which caused the difficulty of procuring labour.

There has been another potent cause of the sufferings which the West Indian islands have undergone. Misgovernment, above all, the mismanagement of

their fiscal affairs, have, in the opinion of those most
intimate with them, had a vast deal to do with their
distresses.   We shall exhibit this more fully in de-
lineating the state of the islands one by one.   We
shall show how swiftly some of them have burst into
the bloom of great prosperity, the moment an improvement was made in their financial arrangements.
We shall show how grievous a drawback the want of
such reforms has been to Jamaica and other islands.
But now we will content ourselves with referring to
one or two somewhat amusing facts: one, that in
Montserrat, according to Dr. Davy, there were but
eighty-five persons who at once were — twenty years
of age, able to read, and payers of direct taxes. Yet
there is a President, a Council, a House of Assembly,
and seventy-seven officials, including the M.P.'s.
There is a Vice-Chancellor, an Attorney-General, a
Solicitor-General, a Queen's Counsel, and so forth.
No wonder that the little community was much in
the case of Frederick the Great's baby brother, who
was " crushed to death by the weighty dress you put
upon it at christening time, especially by the little
crown it wore, which had left a visible black mark
on the poor soft infant's brow."*   Furthermore the
Governor of one of the islands officially explains why
the Assembly has fallen off in number from forty-four
to forty-two, by this rather queer circumstance, that
the *one constituent* who should have elected *two members* for his district, had gone to England.   Truly, a
Reform Bill is needed there, if not here!

* Carlyle, vol. ii. p. 26.

We must here pause for a moment. We have, we
think, shown that it was the loss of monopoly, not
the loss of slavery, which brought the West Indies
to such a crash. Are we then to conclude that though
Slavery is acquitted, Free Trade stands condemned?
Is the history of the West Indies to throw a shield
over the falling cause of Protection?

Quite the reverse. We shall show, ere we have
done, what great wealth Free Trade has already
begun to shower on the West Indies. It may be said,
however, that though in the long run freedom of
trade has shown itself their true friend, yet that at
its outset it was a frightful calamity. But we must
remember that the case of the West Indies was
wholly distinct from that of any nation which should
adopt Free Trade for itself. A nation in so doing
would simply say, " Instead of barring out the good
things of the world by force of law, I will let every-
body who likes pour them into my garners." This
can never, even from the first moment, have any
other effect but that of making that country richer
and happier. But, in the case of the West Indies, it
was quite another thing. There, a small group of
islands had hitherto been assured of a sale of their
produce to the mother-country, without any foreign
competition. To them the resolve of the mother-
country to buy in the open market, instead of buying
from them, was of course a heavy blow for a time.
If the world had never bought guns except at Birmingham, and then suddenly resolved to buy them
wherever they were to be found, why, plainly for a
time, the gunmakers of Birmingham would be in a

F

bad way. That was an exactly parallel case. The overthrow of a monopoly is of vast good to the world in general: to the monopolist it may for a while be ruin

We must remember, too, how unfair a competition was that which was brought to bear by the Act of 1846. The people of Brazil and Cuba not merely had great multitudes of slaves, but they had the slave-trade too, which was actually pouring 150,000 slaves every year into these two countries.* It is allowed, on all hands, that the Cuban planters work their slaves to death, on an average, in seven years. They work night and day during the whole of crop time: *and the losses are made good from Africa.* Clearly, the British planter was not placed in a fair position, when exposed to such a competition. Slavery alone, we are persuaded, would be beaten in a very few years by free labour. But slavery, when the slaves can be worked to death, and new ones got in their stead, is, indeed, a powerful antagonist.

And yet, with all this, the free trader may fairly triumph. It was naturally said in 1846, and it is often said now, that free labour must go to the wall when exposed to such a competition. And yet the sugar returns show, that the import of free-labour sugar, from all free-labour countries, into the United Kingdom, amounted in the ten years ending with 1846, to 41,903,326 cwt. In the ten years ending with 1856, it reached 54,616,229 cwt.! showing that

---

* In 1839, at any rate, Sir Fowell Buxton demonstrated this to be the case, from a great mass of evidence, chiefly official. We need hardly remind the reader that Brazil has since given up the slave trade, but it still is carried on by Cuba.

free labour holds its own, and gains rapidly,— gains an increase of 12,712,903 cwt.—even under such a severe trial. And, so far as the mother-country is concerned, her consumption of sugar has increased, under the reduced duties, from 18,253,111 cwt. in the four years ending with 1846, to 30,470,354 cwt. in the four years ending with 1858.* And, what is most remarkable (and should be well noted by financiers), not only has free trade made this vast addition to the comfort of the people, but the revenue arising from sugar has *increased under the lowered duties*, from 17,750,847*l.* in the four years referred to above, up to 20,883,583*l.* in the four years ending with 1858.†

And now let us bid adieu to "the dreadful past." Those times, thank God, are clean gone for ever. Never again in the West Indies will the hand of man be chained, or his industry cramped, by the law of England. That wickedness, that folly, is dead: and the misery they caused, that, too, is over. The anguish of the slave, his cry of "Think me no man?" as his flesh was torn by the lash, is heard no more. His former owner, impoverished, broken-hearted, has passed away. The old order has given place to new. But here we come to the main question of all, — to the question, Was that crash of 1847 but a passing hurricane, or was it the beginning of an unchangeable doom? Are the West Indies ruined? Was their knell sounded by the philanthropists and

* The consumption per head of the population was 17 lbs. in 1844, and 35¾ lbs. in 1858,—more than twice as much!

† Statistical Tables, published in the "Economist" of January 15, 1859.

free-traders, who broke the slave's bonds, and stripped
those islands of Protection?   Is it true that the West
Indies are, year by year, sinking deeper and deeper
into barbarism and poverty, or has the groundwork
been laid of a great and sound well-being?

But for the irresistible force of the official reports
and statistics we shall bring forward, we might
hardly dare to utter our reply.   So little has the eye
of this country been drawn to the West Indies since
the time of their tribulation, that few are aware of
what has been since going on; and the world does
not dream but that, as their groans are no longer
heard, they are silent in death.   And yet, in truth,
the West Indies are rising with great speed to a
height of wealth, happiness, and comfort unknown to
them before.   The two great experiments, the experiment of emancipation and the experiment of free trade,
have been followed by a success which, for a while, was
dashed with disappointment, but which, year by year,
is growing more and more decisive.   The application
of sound principles, though it may have hastened a
catastrophe which could not have been long delayed;
though, as Mr. Bigelow says, it " precipitated a
result which was inevitable," yet now is bringing our
sugar islands round to a state of high prosperity.

We have already remarked that, when the artificial compulsion which had concentrated almost the
whole labouring force of the slave colonies on the
one work of sugar-making, — when that artificial
compulsion was taken away, there could not fail to
be a redistribution of labour.   We have pointed out
that it was desirable, as well as inevitable, that a

variety of work should take the place of that same-
ness. In fact, the free-trader condemns Protection on
that very ground (amongst others), that it sets men
to work at one kind of production, in lieu of those
other kinds for which the soil and the climate would
be more fit. We should not, therefore, have felt any
disappointment had other occupations almost wholly
displaced the production of the old staples. It would
not have been the smallest proof that our islands
were ruined. It might have come from a wiser and
more profitable employment of labour. This, however, has not been the result. Strangely enough,
freedom of labour and of trade has not lessened but
has actually increased the production of sugar in our
former slave colonies ! In the last two clear years of
slavery (1832 and 1833), they exported to Great
Britain, 8,471,744 cwt. In the two years 1856, 1857,
they exported to Great Britain alone, 8,736,654 cwt.*
And, besides that, a large trade, altogether new, has
sprung up with Australia, the United States, and
other countries, of which we have no account.

And more striking still is the result if we leave out
the one island of Jamaica, whose mismanagement and
financial disorders (as we shall show farther on) have
clogged her grievously. Passing by that one island,
and taking into account the other sixteen, we find
that, whereas in the last six years of slavery they
exported on an average 3,007,782 † cwt. of sugar, in
the last four years Great Britain alone has received

* Sugar Return, 1858.
† This average is given in " The State of the West Indies in
1855," a Colonial-Office document, not published, p. 19.

from them 4,055,521 cwt.*, besides their new trade to
foreign lands.

To this it may be objected, that we take in Mauritius, which had the advantage of a large importation
of Coolies, by whom the sugar is mainly produced.
That is true. But it is to be borne in mind that the
influx of free labour is exactly one of those advantages of which a land is debarred by slavery. It is
a part of the curse of slavery that it repels the free
man. Thus in Italy, under the Emperors, free labour
became extinguished. The whole soil was cultivated by slaves ; and so again Olmsted, in his invalu-
able works on the Slave States and Texas, has shown
how completely slavery has turned aside the torrent
of free labour, which would else have spread over
and fertilised those regions. When then we are told
that to judge of the effect of emancipation we must
exclude those colonies that imported Coolies, we reply at once that this useful importation has been one
of the many blessings that freedom has brought in
her train. But waiving this, and excluding the
Mauritius as well as Jamaica, the remaining fifteen
sugar islands † produced in the last three years
(1855-6-7) 7,427,618 cwt., against 7,405,849 in the
last three years of slavery.‡ So too with rum. Without referring to the Mauritius (whose export has increased to 150 times its former amount !), the export
of rum from all the West Indies, except Jamaica, has

* Sugar Return.

† Antigua, Barbadoes, Dominica, Grenada, Montserrat,
Nevis, St. Kitt's, St. Lucia, St. Vincent, Tobago, Tortola,
Trinidad, Bahamas, Demerara, Berbice.

‡ Return of Sugar and Rum, 1818.

increased from 2,722,880 gallons, under slavery, to 4,674,602 gallons under freedom.*

It is plain then that, as regards seventeen out of the eighteen islands, more wealth is produced, even of that particular species which might have been expected to fall off.

From Jamaica, and from Jamaica alone, the accounts continue to be discouraging. Those received in 1853 and 1854, after the terrible devastation of the cholera and small-pox, were very painful indeed. It is natural to ask why, when every other colony is rapidly rising to prosperity, why should this island, the finest and most important of all, be still in a depressed condition? Nor is this question easily answered. In other of the West-Indian colonies there is a superabundance of waste land. The other colonies have had to contend with the difficulties of encumbered estates, absentee proprietors, and a great fall in the price of produce. The other colonies have had their slaves set free, and have had to buy labour as best they could. Why should Jamaica be still deep under water, while they are swimming gaily? We cannot discover any specific cause which has operated there but did not operate in other colonies, except it be the superlative badness of its government. "There is," says Sir C. Grey, "no system or consistency whatever in the conduct of the financial affairs of the colony, nor any recognised organ of government or legislature which has the power to bring about effective and comprehensive improvements."†

* Return of Sugar and Rum, 1818.
† Papers relative to Jamaica, 1854, p. 6.

Though giving full weight to the difficulty arising from the want of labour,

"I am persuaded," says Sir H. Barkly, "that the want of mutual confidence in the transactions of every-day life, and the insecurity of property arising from the inadequacy of the existing arrangements for enforcing the law, are at the root of the evils which are shaking society in this island to its basis."

These disorders, however, have been in some degree corrected in the last few years. The financial and other affairs of the colony are no longer managed by the whole Assembly, but by a committee, and the members of the Assembly have no longer the pernicious power of initiating money votes, except under the authority of the Governor. The report states that in spite of a very factious and troublesome opposition at the onset, the new Act has been got into successful operation ; and the effect already is visible in rapid improvement. The *exports* of the island rose from 837,276*l.* in 1853, up to 1,003,325*l.* in 1855, being an increase of 166,049*l.* in two years.

Even Jamaica then is making some steps forward; but still it is far outrun by the other islands. Though a catalogue *raisonné* of them may seem dull, yet we feel it to be of so much consequence to show how thoroughly freedom of labour and trade is working out the most beneficial results, that we shall venture to give a series of extracts from the Governors' reports, describing the state and prospects of each colony. But lest it should be thought that these extracts are carefully culled to produce a particular impression, and that if the reader had the whole reports before him he would find complaints and lamentations, we may at once say, that they appear to us to be fair samples of the views entertained by the Governors, and also by other gentlemen intimate with the West Indies. The language of complaint is no longer heard. Throughout these colonies hope and congratulation seem to have taken the place of irritation and despair.

"*Antigua.* — Satisfactory evidence is afforded, by the revenue returns, of increase in trade and mercantile business, consequent upon the revival of agricultural prosperity.*

"*Bahamas.* — The rapidity with which these islands are advancing is indicated by the fact, that the exports and imports rose from 201,497*l.* in 1854, to 304,421*l.* in 1855, an increase of 102,924*l.* in one year. Twenty-three vessels were built in the colony in the year 1855.† The Governor refers to the 'great and important change for the better' in the condition of the people, which he mainly attributes to improved education.‡

"*Barbadoes.* — 'Vast increase of trade.' 'So far the success of cultivation by free labour in Barbadoes is unquestionable.' 'In 1851 more sugar shipped from this island than in any one year since it has been peopled; and it is a remarkable fact that there will be more *labourers'* sugar made this year than previously." §

"Sugar exported, 1842   -   -   21,545 hogsheads.
                    1852   -   -   48,785
            Increase   -   -   27,240 "

Dominica. — 1852 : "The revenue affords a most satisfactory proof of the prosperity of the colony." ‖ 1853 : "The steady maintenance of production is full of promise as to the future." ⊥ The exports show a

* Report, 1858.   † Ibid. 1856.   ‡ Ibid. 1851.
§ Ibid. 1852.   ‖ Ibid. 1852.   ⊥ Ibid. 1854.

considerable increase under heads of sugar, rum,
coffee, cocoa, oranges, fruits, hides, hard wood, and
cotton. 1857 : "Very considerable increase in revenue, and an equally marked improvement in the
amount of imports." The Governor also dwells on
the industry of the bulk of the population, and
on the great amount of general comfort and independence among the labouring class, in which their industry has resulted.*

" The native labourer, whose growing independence,
manifested in the ' small patches of canes and little wooden
mills here and there dotting the chequered plain around,'
the significance of which was so pointedly alluded to in the
last despatch of your Excellency's predecessor, has risen a
step higher, and we now see him becoming the lessee of
large sugar plantations regularly established, with all the
usual appliances. As witness, for example, the lessee of
Hope Vale Estate, containing 492 acres, with water-mill
and works complete ; the lessee of Perseverance Estate,
containing 522 acres, with steam-engine and other appa-
ratus complete ; and the lessee of Mount Hardman, formerly a sugar estate, and lately a cattle farm, with 400
acres of pasture and wood, soon to be revived into its
former state of flourishing luxuriance. True, these were
abandoned properties belonging to absent and needy proprietors, who had not the means of keeping up the cultivation, and were glad to concede them on mere nominal
terms ; but in the course of time the properties will im-
prove without any cost to the owners, while they furnish
the means of profitable employment to, and engage the en-
terprise of, an aspiring class. It is cases like these that the
more intelligent labourer is laying himself out for ; and as
he can manage more economically than his educated land-

* Ibid. 1858.

lord, he spends less, and, saves more ; and, when he cannot find a friend to assist him with pecuniary advances, he procures the physical help of his fellow-labourers, and at harvest either shares the produce or remunerates them from the proceeds of the sale. Even the 'old established hands,' who find it difficult to struggle against the tide, are now emulating the despised 'wooden mills,' and gladly take the canes of their own labourers and neighbouring petty settlers, and manufacture them on the share system, in order to make up something like a return of produce on their ancient patrimony."

From *Grenada* we hear that " contentment appears to pervade all classes of the community.* "A proprietary body of considerable magnitude and importance has already risen from the labouring class." " State of the finances most satisfactory," — owing to augmentation in the imports. Some remarks on the want of labour, but the trade of the island rose in the last two years of which we have returns, from 205,282*l.* to 293,696*l.*, an increase of 88,414*l.*†

In the " Times " of October 15. 1858, the Grenada Report is that "a greatly extended surface is covered by (sugar) cultivation." A considerable increase is noted in the exports of sugar, rum, and cocoa.

It has been urged on the people of Grenada by Mr. Thomson Hankey to abolish all tonnage and import duties, and make all taxation direct ; but at present they have not adopted this sensible advice.

" A class of peasant proprietors and renters of land has come into existence, which in its degree is making rapid strides in prosperity and independence, and a new class of

* Report, 1858.   † Ibid. 1852.

tradesmen more fitted to supply its limited wants than the
larger mercantile firms. But with the change in their
position the peasantry of Grenada have hitherto altered
but very slightly their simple habits of life, and conse-
quently their purchases of imported goods for personal
consumption do not suffice to fill up the void that has been
created. As they advance in civilisation as well as in material well-being, they will no doubt become consumers on
a more extended scale, but the present tariff being adapted
to a different state of things, operates to check this deve-
lopment."

Guiana. — None of the West Indies have gone
through a harder struggle. "The fall of prices in
1847 and 1848 was so sudden and so enormous as to
have almost annihilated the colony at that crisis,"
writes the Governor in 1852 (?) ; but he goes on to
state, that now "the revenue is flourishing, population augmenting, education spreading, crime diminishing, and trade increasing."

Montserrat. — After referring to "the improved
and improving state of the community, as allowed on
all hands," and giving various details, the Governor *
says, "So much for the increase of confidence, enter-
prise, and industry in Montserrat." "No island in
these seas exhibits a more decisive tendency to social
and moral regeneration and improvement. The rural
population are quiet, contented, and orderly. Their
condition one of great comfort." A new system of
taxation (as we understand, throwing it off imports
upon real property) came into operation in June,
1856, and with such striking and powerful effect, that

* Ibid. 1853.

the imports more than doubled in value in the course of the year !

Nevis. — The case of this island is peculiarly interesting, because in it an experiment has been tried in taxation, which may perhaps some day become generally adopted throughout the world. Things in Nevis had got to such a desperate state — they were, in fact, past all bearing — that at last Mr. President Seymour, a gentleman of remarkable boldness and vigour, induced the legislature to consent to a radical change in the fiscal system. The import duties were totally abolished : and a tax of 20 per cent placed on rentals.

Small as the field was in which this experiment was tried, its astonishing results are worth noting by statesmen. The new system came into play, March, 1856. In that year the imports rose from 19,728*l.* to 34,449*l.* New shops were speedily opened. House-rent rose threefold. The sound of the hammer was heard, and the smell of fresh paint experienced, where all had been crumbling decay. " The roads appear as if the greater part of the population had new clothed themselves, and in the harbour, so often deserted, I now count, ten ships of considerable burden." *

* Report, 1857. President Rumbold, who succeeded President Seymour, disapproved of the change, on account of the greater difficulty of raising revenue by direct taxation. He says, however, that " there appears now to be at work an industrious spirit of improvement : cultivation appears to be carefully attended to.   .   .   .   There is ample room to hope for the gradual regeneration of the colony."

St. Kitts. — "A larger quantity of sugar is produced now than in the time of slavery " * (though on
a smaller area). " The agricultural prospects of the
island are most encouraging. Its financial condition
continues satisfactory ; so do the Education Returns.
The whole trade increased from 246,536*l.* in 1856,
to 352,769*l.* in 1857, — an increase of 106,233*l.* in one
year ! Attendance in schools steadily increasing † ;
crime steadily diminishing." ‡

St. Lucia. — " At no period in her history was
there a greater breadth of land under sugar cultivation, than at the present moment." §   The Education
Returns are " on the whole extremely satisfactory."
There seems to the Governor to be an increasing
desire on the part of a very respectable ‖ portion of
the inhabitants to avail themselves of the schools.
In 1857, the Administrator notes the extension of
cane cultivation ⫦ ; and says that " the aspect of the
country is more promising : the prospects of the agriculturist are encouraging."

" Exports of sugar 1838—1842 - 4,588,475 hogsheads.
     1852—1856 - 6,392,093
   Increase -   -   - 1,803,618

St. Vincent. — In 1852 the Governor described the
financial management as " inexcusable."   In 1856
important reforms were made. The result is, that
in 1857 he says, " It is matter of great satisfaction to

* Report, 1856.   † Ibid. 1858.
‡ Ibid. 1856.   § Ibid. 1853.
‖ In the sense of a very large portion.
⫦ Report, 1852.

me to state that . . . the foundation has been laid for
a great and progressive improvement." He speaks of
extended cultivation, and of " a really sound and
healthy state of the colony at present, and a cheering
and promising prospect for the future." He says the
condition of the labourer is almost universally one of
comfort; and describes the rising villages, the growing number of freeholders and leaseholders, and the
steady progressive increase in the value of imports.*

In 1858 he describes the colony as in a "most
satisfactory" state. " Agricultural operations largely
extended ;" his anticipation of its continued progress
and prosperity had been fully realised. Imports and
exports had increased from 249,526l. in 1856, to
406,159l. in 1857; an increase of 156,633l. in one
year.† And he expressly attributes it to " increased
cultivation and prosperity." He says, " the cheerful
prospects of 1856 are being fully realised. The present position of St. Vincent is most satisfactory, and
its future most promising."

In *Tobago*, again, the accounts were dismal in 1852
and 1853, which the Governor said was beyond doubt
owing to the state of its financial affairs. In 1856,
however, an improved system having been adopted,
the result is, that already the Governor " has much
satisfaction in taking a more encouraging view of the
prospects of the colony."‡ A marked improvement
is visible in the revenue returns. The labourers are
described as well behaved and industrious.§

Tortola under slavery exported 15,559 cwt. of

* 1857.   † 1858.   ‡ Ibid.   § Ibid.

sugar. It now exports none at all. But the change is wholly an advantage. The island is singularly suitable for the raising of stock, and accordingly "all the people, with few exceptions, are owners of cattle, which they dispose of to great advantage."

It is very gratifying to be able to observe that the labouring population appear fully sensible of the advantages of education to their children, and that the latter manifest a great desire to benefit by the opportunity afforded them.

Trinidad is highly flourishing. The whole trade has increased from a yearly average under slavery of 810,636*l.*, to 1,239,241*l.* in 1856, an increase of 428,605*l.* In 1852 the crop was the largest ever shipped from the island ; and it has been extending since, — "marked improvement in the cultivation of the sugar estates."* Export of sugar rose from an average of 310,797 cwt. under slavery, to 426,042 in the seven years ending 1854.

" The crop for this year is the largest ever shipped, and there is every probability of a considerable increase next year."

These specific accounts of the several islands are borne out by the statistics and reports that relate to our West Indies *en masse.* To men of business, one fact will seem almost enough by itself to show their sound commercial state, namely, that in the year 1857 the Colonial Bank received bills from the West Indies to the amount of more than 1,300,000*l.*, and less than

* 1853.

8000*l.* were returned.* Nor was there a single
failure in the West-India trade during the frightful
commercial crisis in the autumn of that year. And,
as a demonstration that the West Indies are advancing
with great rapidity, we may give a few statistics,
which simply show that trade and agriculture are
expanding year by year: —

Imports of Britain from the West Indies.

Coffee, 1857 - - - - - - 4,056,379 lbs.
    Five preceding years (average) - 3,177,834

        Increase - - - - - 878,545

Cotton wool, 1857 - - - - - 1,443,568
    Five preceding years (average) - 478,894

        Increase - - - - - 964,674

Again, taking a wider area:

Sugar, 1858 - - - - - - 3,385,007 cwt.

    Seven years since   1850 (average)   3,063,254
    Ten   „   preceding „ (average)   2,606,135

        Annual Increase   - - - 457,119

Rum,
    Seven years since   1850 (average) 6,066,226 galls.
    Ten   „   preceding „ (average) 4,514,513

        Annual Increase   - - - 1,551,693

* See Report of Colonial Bank, for June 30, 1857.

Cocoa,

Seven years ending 1850 (average)   4,158,439 lbs.

Ten   „   preceding „   (average)   2,590,681

Annual Increase   -   -   -   1,567,758

The total exports from Great Britain to the West
Indies in 1857 were valued at half a million * more
than the average of the preceding ten years, and actually in that year exceeded her exports to Sweden,
Norway, Denmark, Greece, Azores, Madeira, and
Morocco, all combined.† The exports and imports
together of the West Indies amounted, in the four
years ending with 1853, to just 32,500,000*l*.; and in
the four years ending with 1857, to just 37,000,000*l*.,
an increase of 4,500,000*l*. in four years. In the year
1857 the total trade to and fro of these islands was
valued at 10;735,000*l*., and (as noted above) the value
of the sugar imported from them into the United
Kingdom, in that year, was no less than 5,618,000*l*.!
These official statistics and reports absolutely de-
monstrate the fact that the West Indies are rapidly
advancing in wealth and prosperity; nor must it be
supposed that they are merely " putting money in
their purse," without a corresponding advance in the
general character of the people. After the great

* 1857   -   -   -   - £2,349,787.
  Ten years before (average) -   - 1,861,260.

† Trade and Navigation Accounts, 1858.
  Exports to those seven countries - £2,348,000.
    „   to the West Indies   - 2,349,787.

crash of 1847, indeed, when society was flung into
misery and confusion, the extreme want of capital for
a while had a demoralising effect upon the labourer ;
and we believe that during that period there was far
more idleness and vice than at any other time since
slavery was done away. But it is plain that an ex-
traordinary improvement has taken place in the
habits, and character, and position of the negroes in
the West Indies. The contrast between the whole
life of the labourer in these islands, and what it was
when he was a slave, is in the highest degree striking.
We have already portrayed some of the features of
the old state. We have referred to the frightful
tyranny to which he was liable, the severe punishments, and the waste of life; and unless the proprietor had been resident on the estate, and had taken
pains to make things better, the slaves seem to have
lived in a miserable style. There were many exceptions, of course ; and the *domestic* slaves were often
able to make as grand a display as the freemen now ;
but for the most part a hut of wattle, daubed with
mud, was the home, and a coarse cap, shirt, and
trousers formed the dress, of the prædial slaves ; the
females being arrayed in a shift and coarse baize pet-
ticoat, with a handkerchief round their heads. Their
food, too (consisting in a great degree of salt fish),
was mainly dependent on the caprice or ability of
their owners, and was but too often far short of what
they required.

The change from the old state of things is described
on all hands as being most gratifying ; and especially
in those thousands of cases where the negroes have

built altogether new villages for themselves. The
cottages are either neatly thatched, or shingled with
pieces of hard wood. Some are built of stone or
wood; but generally are plastered also on the outside,
and whitewashed. Many are ornamented with a
portico in front, to screen the sitting-apartment from
sun and rain; while for the admission of light and
air, as well as to add to their appearance, they exhibit
either shutters or jalousies, painted green, or small
glass windows.

" There is usually a sleeping-apartment at each end and
a sitting-room in the centre. The floors are in most instances terrased, although boarded ones for sleeping-rooms
are becoming common. Many of the latter contain good
mahogany bedsteads, a washing-stand, a looking-glass, and
chairs. The middle apartment is usually furnished with a
sideboard, displaying sundry articles of crockery-ware,
some decent-looking chairs, and not unfrequently with a
few broadsheets of the Tract Society hung round the walls
in neat frames of cedar. For cooking food, and other domestic purposes, a little room or two is erected at the back
of the cottage, where are also arranged the various conve-
niences for keeping domestic stock. The villages are laid
out in regular order, being divided into lots more or less
intersected by roads or streets. The plots are usually in
the form of an oblong square. The cottage is situated at
an equal distance from each side of the allotment, and at
about eight or ten feet from the public thoroughfare. The
piece of ground in front is, in some instances, cultivated in
the style of a European garden; displaying rose-bushes,
and other flowering shrubs, among the choicer vegetable
productions; while the remainder is covered with all the
substantial vegetables and fruits of the country hetero-
geneously intermixed."

The result is, that they present "a very pleasing appearance." Sir Henry Barkly was reminded by those in the hills of the villages in Switzerland*, and he says they have a decided air of progressive civilisation and comfort about them; and that it is quite clear, whatever may be the case elsewhere, that their inhabitants are not retrograding either in their moral or physical condition.† And the same despatch contains a report by a stipendiary magistrate, and speaks of "the thousands of well cultivated settlements, with their tastefully arranged cottages and gardens, which have given quite a different appearance to the country since August, 1838, and bespeak the prosperity and comfort of the occupants, and present a cheering prospect, and an encouraging hope for the future."‡ Another magistrate reports to him that the advancement in the condition of the labouring class is unmistakably apparent.

"The peasantry, who were formerly unused to domestic comfort and a state of independence, are now otherwise circumstanced. A very large number of them are owners of freehold properties, on which they are comfortably located. They also own a large number of horses, hogs, and other live stock. They trade extensively in the native products of the parish, which they cultivate in such abundance, that boats are constantly conveying cargoes of yams, cocoas, and plantains to the port of Falmouth in the parish of Trelawney, where they are scarce, and in great demand.

* See Antigua and the Antiguans; Philippo's Jamaica, &c. &c.; Sir H. Barkly's Journal in 1853, (P. P.) Despatch, May, 1854.
† Sir H. Barkly, 1854, P.P. ‡ Ibid. Appendix.

The vessels employed in this traffic are almost exclusively their own property. The degrading practice of concubinage has been forsaken by a large number, who have embraced the marriage state, and the weekly publication of intended matrimonial alliances is proof that matrimony among them is on the increase. They contribute more largely than any other class to the general taxation of the parish, and not a few enjoy and exercise electoral rights. Generally they may be said to be a fair specimen of the labouring people of this island; willing and tractable, civil and obedient, confiding in those who employ them, often toiling on estates for weeks and months in expectation of reward, but in many instances ill-requited for their confidence and labour by disappointment and non-payment."

The number of such settlements that have been established since emancipation is almost incredible. Within eight years of that event, nearly two hundred villages of the kind we have been describing had been built, and full 100,000 acres of land purchased, by the negroes of Jamaica alone. A statement was read in the House of Commons in 1842, by Lord Stanley (then Colonial Minister), that "it would appear wonderful how so much had been accomplished in the island, in building, planting, digging, and making fences. The number of freeholders *who have become freeholders by their accumulation and industry*, in the Island of Jamaica, amounted, in 1840, to 7,340." *

It is usual to fancy that the free negroes desert the estates to squat upon wild lands; but, although this has occasionally been the case, by far the greater

* See Hansard's Debates (?), and Philippo's Jamaica, p. 228.

number of them have bought land, and that at a good
price, for their settlements. And the negro proprietor
is just as proud of his own home and freehold as any
Englishman might be. The names they give them
may be taken as a slight indication of their feelings:
" Content my own," " Comfort Castle," " Happy Hut,"
" Thank God to see it," and so forth. One is men-
tioned by the Rev. Mr. Philippo, as being entitled
" Occasion call," which the owner explained thus:
" If any person have business wid me, him can come
in ; but if him don't want me in pottickler, me no
wants him company, and him no 'casion to come."

In appearance very many of the negroes have by
no means a disagreeable exterior. In fact the clever
authoress of " Antigua and the Antiguans " declares
that many of the creole * negroes may be termed very
goodlooking. High and well-formed foreheads, black
and sparkling eyes, aquiline noses, and lips with only
a slight pout, are not uncommon, though others of the
same race are more like apes than human beings.
Both men and women, she tells us, are seldom to be
seen except in the most becoming attire ; the dress of
the women generally consisting of a printed or cotton
gown, with a white handkerchief tied round their
heads like a turban, and a neat straw hat trimmed
with white riband. But on high days and festivals,
it must be owned that the splendour of the negro
array is not in the purest taste. One of the writers
on the West Indies was shocked by seeing a negress
who actually was adorned with pink stockings, yellow

* *i. e.* native: not imported from Africa.

shoes, and a bonnet of green trimmed with pink, and displaying a blue rose with silver leaves! Silks, satins, muslins, and crapes are plentifully used, and even the " gentlemen " will come out on occasion in a truly glorious costume; with velvet collars, radiant waistcoats, and boots expressly made to " stamp and creak " well.   They all carry umbrellas, silk if possible; and pocket-handkerchiefs, with one end making its appearance from the coat pocket.   We are told, however, that the love for gaudy colours is disappearing; and that modesty and sensibility are becoming increasingly apparent in the female sex.   In their names, the march of intellect has extinguished the Sambos, Pompeys, and Darkeys of former days, and now the shining pickaninnies rejoice in the appellations of " Adeline Floretta," " Rosalind Monimia," " Alonzo Frederick," and so forth.   One cannot but smile at these little affectations; but all this shows a progress towards refinement and civilisation, though some of its offshoots are laughable.   The same may be said of their manners, in which a surprising improvement has taken place.   " The uncouth address and sullen aspect and carriage of the slaves " has been replaced by a great deal of graceful kindliness and ease towards strangers, and a politeness and respect to each other which may often approach extravagance, but is much better than the rough address so common in many parts of England among the working classes.   No negro peasant meets another without exchanging salutations and inquiries.   Age is particularly venerated, and the noisy little negroes at their sport will stop while one of their old people is passing, with, " How d'ye, ma'm? " and " How d'ye, me picnee? " is the courteous reply. Every one praises their generosity and kindness. To the miserable pauper whites, who abound in the West Indies (and whose squalor and feebleness show the wisdom of Carlyle's expectation, that the West Indies will some day be saved by a population of " true splinters of the old Harz rock, heroic white men, worthy to be called old Saxons " *), they are often known to act the part of guardian angels. They will work for them, feed them, clothe them, without the slightest wish or prospect of receiving remuneration.

They are rising too with rapidity in the social scale, and would seem to be as fit as white men for any kind of employment. Mr. Baird mentions that, in the legislatures of many of the islands, there are already sundry negro members, as well as many gentlemen of colour. When Mr. Bigelow visited Jamaica, there were ten or a dozen coloured men in the Legislative Assembly, which consists altogether of about fifty members; and the police force, the officers of the penitentiary, the officers of the courts of justice, as well as some of the barristers, were coloured men; and we believe they have since been freely admitted to the magistracy and to political office. The old prejudice against African blood is disappearing, though under slavery it was intensely strong; so much so, that the coloured people were generally not allowed to be buried in the same

* Occasional Discourses, p. 22. See Antigua and the An- tiguans, Philippo's Jamaica, Baird's West Indies, &c. &c.

churchyard with the whites. Nay, at St. John's, in
Antigua, the church bell was not allowed to be pro-
faned by tolling for the demise of these degraded
people, and a smaller one was actually provided for
that purpose !

Year by year, too, education is making way ; and
though in some districts it is complained that the
negroes do not show eagerness to obtain schooling for
their children, from others very satisfactory reports
are sent ; and the Governors, almost without exception, state that crime is diminishing in the islands.
In fact, crime of an atrocious character is very rare
indeed. The negroes are guilty of a great deal of
petty pilfering, and they are also regardless of truth ;
but, happily, drunkenness is not one of their prevail-
ing faults ; nor are they given to deeds of violence,
or of deliberate villany. They are a merry, light-
hearted, and kindly people ; somewhat shallow and
thoughtless, and with the faults that come of that
character ; but docile, orderly, and peaceable.

We must now conclude. We trust the reader will
agree with us in thinking that the facts of the case
prove, first, that if emancipation has not worked so
well as it might have done, had due preparation been
made for freedom, this was the fault, not of the
abolitionists, but of the planters. Secondly, that the
lack of labourers has been a trouble and difficulty to
the planters, but has not amounted to a severe
grievance, and has been mainly due to the lack of
capital to pay their wages regularly. Thirdly, that
the crash of 1847 and the ensuing years was not
caused by emancipation; but was caused by the fall

in the price of sugar, consequent on the Act of 1846, and the concurrent events.

Each of these propositions is of importance. But the two main conclusions which are enforced upon us by our investigation are these : the one, that slavery and monopoly were bearing the West Indies to ruin ; the other, that under free labour and free trade they are rising to great wealth. Under slavery and monopoly, the labouring class was miserable, and was perishing miserably. Under slavery and monopoly, the owners of the soil were reduced to the greatest pitch of distress. The state of affairs which had arisen under this old dispensation had rendered a crash some day inevitable. But when once that blow had fallen, and the old things had passed away, and the new things had come, then the inherent virtue of the principle of freedom became manifest ; and it is now working out the most beneficent, the most astonishing — what a few years ago would have seemed the most incredible — results. Wisdom has been justified of her children. Seeking only to do the thing that was just and noble, — seeking not to please herself, but to do the will of God, — England set free her slaves. It is plain that, but for her so doing, her colonies would have sunk to irretrievable destruction. It proves now that, by so doing, she has set them on the way to a prosperity and happiness unknown before ; that not only are the former slaves enjoying a degree of comfort and independence almost unparalleled, but that our own trade with these islands is becoming of higher and higher value. They are yearly enriching us more and more with the wealth of their fertile soil.   Instead of being the plague of statesmen, the disgrace of England, they are becoming possessions to the British Crown of incalculable value.   Never did any deed of any nation show more signally that to do right is the truest prudence, than the great deed of emancipation.

> " Not once or twice, in our rough island story,
>   The path of duty was the path of glory."

And in her dealings with the negro race, both in the West Indies and in Africa, England, having ' only thirsted for the right,' has already begun to find the wisdom of that course.   The fight for freedom has been fought amid great discouragement ; for a time there were heart-breaking drawbacks to the success attained.   But it has been fought with a good courage.   And now the spread of commerce and civilisation in West Africa ; the happiness of the happiest peasants in the world in the West Indies ; the improving agriculture, the extending trade of these islands ; the cheering news which Governor after Governor is sending home of their thriving state, — such is the reward, to her own self, as well as to them, which England is reaping from her generous, self-denying, Christian policy.

THE END.

LONDON
PRINTED BY SPOTTISWOODE AND CO.
NEW-STREET SQUARE.

For EU product safety concerns, contact us at Calle de José Abascal, 56–1°,
28003 Madrid, Spain or eugpsr@cambridge.org.

www.ingramcontent.com/pod-product-compliance
Ingram Content Group UK Ltd.
Pitfield, Milton Keynes, MK11 3LW, UK
UKHW012336130625
459647UK00009B/333